T0322699

A Bird A Day

A Bird A Day

Dominic Couzens

BATSFORD

First published in the United Kingdom in 2020 by
Batsford
43 Great Ormond Street
London WC1N 3HZ
An imprint of B.T. Batsford Holdings Ltd

ISBN: 9781849945868

A CIP catalogue record for this book is available from the British Library.

25 24
10 9 8 7 6 5 4

Reproduction by Rival Colour Ltd, UK
Printed by Toppan Leefung Printing, China

This book can be ordered direct from the publisher at the website:
www.batsfordbooks.com, or try your local bookshop.

CONTENTS

INTRODUCTION

There isn't a day of the year when birds aren't around us, visible and audible. There isn't a day when, assuming our circumstances allow it, we cannot see them and enjoy them – if only briefly out of a window, or the corner of our eye, or as part of our life's soundtrack. Birds are ubiquitous and global. There are only a handful of places in the world where there aren't birds.

This book celebrates that fact. Its real aim is to encourage and inspire people to look at birds, whenever and wherever they can. Hopefully, it can open a window on the wonderful world of birds, because the world of birds is awe-inspiring.

According to the latest official list, compiled by the International Ornithological Congress, there are 10,770 species, plus another 158 that have become extinct since the beginning of the 16th century. That means that there are 10,928 birds that are known to people. That is undoubtedly the tip of the iceberg of the number of species that have evolved since birds first arose about 150 million years ago.

This book celebrates one species a day. It could be 30. Every bird species has a story. You could write this book ten times over and still have interesting stories left. However, for the purpose of actually producing a publication, it has been necessary to be selective, and the 366 species included (including one for the leap year) are hopefully a satisfactory range from the glittering array available.

The process of selection has various stages. Some birds pick themselves; if you had to pick, say, 366 actors, then some are so famous or charismatic, or currently fascinating, that you couldn't possibly leave them out. So it is with a bird such as an ostrich – unique, iconic and world famous. It's the same for albatrosses and penguins and birds of paradise.

Other species you cannot leave out include those that have a place in our cultures, so they are significant for our interactions with them. These are many and varied but include birds we consume and hunt, species such as chickens (red junglefowl), turkeys and grouse, those in literature (poems, stories) and those that are intimately wrapped up in our different lives and cultures – emus to aboriginal Australians, common loons to native Americans and peafowl to Hindus, among many others. Some of their cultural stories are told in this book.

Opposite: A
keel-billed toucan
(*Ramphastos
sulfuratus*)
encounters a
montezuma
oropendola
(*Psarocolius
montezuma*) in
Costa Rica.

Below: Parrots.
Chromo-
lithograph 1896.

Some birds are scientifically significant. The last few decades have
been awash with pioneering research, and the advent of such advances
as DNA fingerprinting and satellite tracking have unveiled many
remarkable facts. Birds do extraordinary things and their lives are
much more complicated that anyone imagined 40 years ago. Many
of the best discoveries are included in this book.

Of course, in a particular book like this you must also include
characters that are seasonally significant. Birds have seasonal resonance
– just think of the arrival of a swallow in the northern hemisphere
in spring, and then of the same bird in the southern hemisphere in
their spring. Think of geese and cranes arriving in autumn to various
points around the globe. Think of the swelling of bird songs in the
rainy season in the tropics, or before the monsoon. Around the world,
the arrival of certain birds in certain places has heralded delight and
understanding. Throughout this book I have tried to place birds
on appropriate days, with migratory movements, song delivery or
breeding signs in mind.

Finally, there are some birds that remind us that our world is in dire need of conserving. Sprinkled through the book are stories of endangered birds, some with unhappy endings, but many with ongoing hope. I have included some anniversaries of extinction dates, but also some where a species' fortunes turned.

As we all know, though, our earth is changing, and the danger to all life on earth has become apparent, through climate change and many other factors. There is a real possibility that some of the seasonal resonance of bird arrivals and departures will diminish in the future.

So there are many reasons to include a bird in this book, but perhaps the most important is to heighten knowledge and respect for wild creatures in general. The future of birds on this planet partly depends on conservationists winning the hearts and minds of people around the world, so that they can accept the political and cultural changes that will help save the environment. If a book like this can make a very small contribution towards more people loving birds, it will have been worth writing.

RED-CROWNED CRANE
Grus japonensis

A pair of red-crowned cranes dance the New Year away in Hokkaido, Japan. The species also breeds in China.

It's the New Year, a time when we all hope for peace and longevity. No bird symbol represents these quite like the red-crowned crane, a bird steeped in the culture of the Far East. For centuries it has been depicted in art and legend.

In China, the red-crowned crane represents immortality. In Japan, it was once believed that it could live for 1,000 years. It is also a symbol of fidelity; the cranes do indeed mate for life.

These days the red-crowned crane is a rare bird, with a world population of only around 3,000. The longevity of the species itself is far from assured.

COMMON KESTREL
Falco tinnunculus

The common kestrel hovers over open ground everywhere from western Europe to far-eastern Russia. Small mammals are the main prey.

For the sheer joy of observation, and the sheer joy of language leaping in all directions, it is hard to top Gerard Manley Hopkins' description of a kestrel in 'The Windhover', a poem he wrote in Wales (UK) in 1877.

I caught this morning morning's minion, king-
    dom of daylight's dauphin, dapple-dawn-drawn Falcon, in his riding
    Of the rolling level underneath him steady air, and striding
High there, how he rung upon the rein of a wimpling wing
In his ecstasy! then off, off forth on swing,
    As a skate's heel sweeps smooth on a bow-bend: the hurl and gliding
    Rebuffed the big wind. My heart in hiding
Stirred for a bird – the achieve of, the mastery of the thing!

The kestrel hovers in just this way above open ground, searching for its staple diet, small mammals.

WANDERING ALBATROSS
Diomedea exulans

Now is the middle of the egg-laying period for wandering albatrosses on the few islands where they breed in the southern oceans.

King of the Roaring Forties, the wandering albatross rides out the wrath of the Southern Oceans with barely a wingbeat. With a 3.5m (11½ft) wingspan, the greatest of any bird, the albatross is perfectly adapted for gliding, its slender wing shape promoting lift and reducing drag. It can travel enormous distances over the oceans, expending little or no energy, harnessing the power of the wind and the waves. It routinely travels 2,000km (1,250 miles) just to go foraging for its young in the nest.

Recent radio tracking has shown that parents foraging from the sub-antarctic Crozet Islands in the Indian Ocean (46°S) go in search of food in different directions: the males go south and clockwise, the females north and anti-clockwise.

GOLDEN EAGLE
Aquila chrysaetos

A remarkably widespread and successful eagle, inhabiting much of North America and Eurasia, mainly wild, treeless country.

These magnificent birds of prey inhabit huge tracts of wild, remote country, where they terrorize a wide range of prey, from medium-sized birds such as grouse, to mammals like rabbits and hares. It is claimed that they can spot a mountain hare from a distance of 2km (1¼ miles), such is their visual acuity.

These birds use a variety of techniques for hunting. One of the more remarkable is to chase large animals to a place of great peril – so, for example, they might corner a young ibex on a precarious rock face, causing the unfortunate animal to lose its footing and fall to its death.

The golden eagle's main foraging technique, however, is flushing, in which the eagle flies low over wild country, following the slopes, hoping to come across prey and surprise it into the open. Pairs of golden eagles practice this method in tandem, one bird performing the flush, the second making the kill.

GREAT TIT
Parus major

Although it's only the beginning of January, throughout Europe male great tits are already in full voice. Their cheerful, breezy 'Teacher, teacher' song chimes across the bare winter woodlands and their brilliant colours are telling. Birds from deciduous woodland, which is high-quality habitat, have brighter breasts than those born in coniferous woodland. The latter is marginal great tit habitat, so those raised there are from the wrong side of the tracks – and, to a potential mate, that shows.

EURASIAN WREN
Troglodytes troglodytes

A strange folk ritual known as Wrenning used to take place in parts of the British Isles and Ireland. People would go out on Twelfth Night (6th January) or St Stephen's Day (26th December), wearing fancy dress and beat the vegetation to flush out a wren. They would catch the wren and either put it in a cage or nail the unfortunate bird to a pole. The captors would then walk from house to house asking for gifts of food and drink in exchange for wren feathers.

MUTE SWAN
Cygnus olor

Above: Mute swans are found in Europe and western Asia; some populations migrate south in winter. Introduced to North America.

Top left: Abundant bird of Europe, the Middle East, central and northern Asia.

Bottom left: A songbird of dense vegetation in Europe and Asia.

Swans are magnificent birds, with their crystal clear, white plumage, long necks and marvellous, imperious flight with slow, powerful wing beats. They are among the heaviest of all birds, with a male mute swan weighing in at 10kg (22lb) and a female 8kg (17½lb). They need a long run, with much foot-pattering, just to take off; the wide-bodied jets of the bird world.

The mute swans is unusual among swans for its relative silence, although it grunts regularly and will make whining sounds. The other swans, however, make loud, bugling or twanging calls, and their flocks are a babble of conversation. No wonder its English common name is 'mute'.

But this swan does have a song, it is just that it is made by its wings. As the bird flies, the primary feathers swish in the air to produce a sweet, rhythmic sighing. This marvellous sound is audible for up to 2km (1¼ miles), so the flock can easily stick together and not bother to open their mouths.

DARK-EYED JUNCO
Junco hyemalis

To many in North America, juncos are the ultimate winter birds. Breeding in the far north, from Alaska to Labrador, they spill south in autumn and gather into flocks that are a familiar sight in backyards, woodlots, parks and suburban areas. Handsome, with their white outer tail feathers and bold plumage, many still refer to them as 'snowbirds', as renowned naturalist and painter John James Audubon did in 1831. They live as many human snowbirds do, taking up winter residence in warmer climes to escape the chill back home.

Juncos (the name is thought to come from *Juncus*, a genus of rushes, although juncos are not birds of wet areas) come in a number of colour forms, especially in the west. These were once recognized as separate species.

Dark-eyed juncos breed across northern and upland parts of North America, in various types of forest; mainly in winter south of the Great Lakes.

ZEBRA FINCH
Taeniopygia guttata

These finches are common across arid regions of Australia and some Indonesian islands; a popular cage bird.

If you're a male zebra finch, a small nomadic bird found in arid parts of Australia and Indonesia, you should be suspicious of the gender of your offspring. If your mate tends to produce females, the chances are that she doesn't think much of you.

Some female birds, including zebra finches, are able to manipulate the sex ratio of their offspring, although how they do this is unknown. If their mate is particularly attractive, they tend to produce more male offspring, since it pays for the father's good genes to be passed on. However, if their mate is nothing special, they produce more female offspring, since there is no point producing yet more inadequate males!

LONG-TAILED TIT
Aegithalos caudatus

These gregarious birds are found in small flocks in woodland all across Europe and Asia as far east as Japan.

On cold nights in January, long-tailed tits huddle tightly together. This close bodily contact means that they lose heat at a slower rate. These long-tailed tit huddles involve family members, including the mother and father, the previous brood and some adult relatives. Surprisingly, the adults take the warmest positions in the centre, leaving their offspring to cope with the chilliest, most perilous spots around the outside of the huddle.

LITTLE PENGUIN
Eudyptula minor

The world's smallest penguin breeds all year round on the sandy and rocky islands and coasts of southern Australia and New Zealand.

It's easier than you think to see a wild penguin. Most people think they are only found in the Antarctic, while some, including film makers, mistakenly believe they live cheek by jowl with polar bears in the Arctic. In fact, any suitably chilly water in the southern hemisphere will do, including around Australia, New Zealand, South Africa and southern South America.

Probably the easiest of all to see are the little penguins found in Australia and New Zealand, where a handful even live wild in Sydney Harbour. There is a permanent viewing platform on Phillip Island, near Melbourne, where visitors can pay to see the birds coming ashore on Summerland Beach.

'Tɪwɪ
Drepanis coccinea

Pronounced 'ee-EE-vee' this vibrant bird uses its curved beak to drink nectar. It can be found on the main islands of Hawaii, Maui and Kauai; all but lost from Molokai and Oahu.

We should be grateful that the gorgeous 'Iiwi still exists in the world. This lovely bird with its crimson plumage, remarkable curved bill and vivacious manner is a member of a group of birds called Hawaiian honeycreepers. Their populations have slumped dramatically since the arrival of human settlers on the remote Hawaiian archipelago. No less than 18 of the 39 recognised species are now extinct.

The biggest cause, besides the usual issue of loss of habitat due to deforestation, has been an unusual one: malaria caused by introduced mosquitoes. Ninety per cent of all 'Iwis bitten by a single infected mosquito die, and 100 per cent of all individuals bitten more than once. Only places above 1,300m (4,250ft), where it is too cold for mosquitoes, remain safe for these birds.

WHITE-WINGED CHOUGH
Corcorax melanorhamphos

Just now the young choughs are hatching and being fed in the open eucalypt woodlands of eastern Australia.

The hardships of the Australian dry country make birds do some very strange things, and none more so than the white-winged choughs.

These birds live in family groups, based on an adult pair and their offspring from previous years. The group defends its territory from neighbouring groups, sometimes violently, and the birds spend each day foraging together on the ground. When it comes to breeding, the adult pair build a nest out of mud, and everybody contributes to raising each year's young.

Raising young is hard, even with co-operation, and the largest groups of choughs have the best chance of success, since these have the most helpers. Because there is a direct relationship between the size of the group and nesting success, some groups resort to extreme measures to increase their flock size. They do so by kidnapping the youngsters from neighbouring groups during disputes!

21

ANDEAN CONDOR
Vultur gryphus

Found all year round in the Andes of South America, from Colombia to Tierra del Fuego, condors can live as long as humans.

The world's largest bird of prey, with a wingspan of up to 3.2m (10½ft) and a weight up to 15kg (33lb), the Andean condor is the last remaining massive scavenging bird in South America. There were once raptors with wingspans up to 6m (19½ft) soaring over the plains here, feeding on the carcasses of prehistoric megafauna while the Andes were still foothills. Nowadays the condor is only rivalled by a few albatrosses, swans and pelicans as the world's largest flying bird of any kind. It soars effortlessly over Andean peaks and patrols the cliffs bordering the oceans. Its huge size, colourful face and gorgeous white-centred wings render it unmistakable.

It looks fierce but is no more than a scavenger, eating the carcasses of large animals, often domestic ones such as sheep or llamas. On the coast, dead sealions or whales suffice.

The condor has been idolised by people for at least 4500 years. In Andean mythology it is associated with the sun god, and the Upper World. In more recent times it has been the object of the remarkable, elemental Yawar Festival, which takes place in many Peruvian villages. A condor is captured and tethered to a bull, the latter of which is knifed to death by the villagers, who set the condor free when the bull expires. The ceremony marks the release of the Andean peoples, represented by the condor, from their Spanish oppressors, represented by the bull.

GREAT CORMORANT
Phalacrocorax carbo

The non-waterproof cormorant has to hang itself out to dry. This successful waterbird is found in Europe, eastern North America, North Africa, parts of Asia and Australia.

Cormorants are water birds that aren't waterproof. At first glance this makes them seem utterly unsuited to a life of immersive fishing, as if they were pilots afraid of flying. The reality, though, is that having feathers that quickly become saturated with water reduces the bird's buoyancy and allows it to pursue fast-moving fish underwater without too much drag. When diving, cormorants hold their wings at their sides and steer using their tail and the webbing of their feet.

The cormorant's dense bones and reduced body fat also ensures that they sink easily; they occasionally swallow stones for the same purpose. However, there is a downside for this saturated bird when it returns to land. It must spend hours holding its wings out to dry – and that, indeed, is often our most familiar image of this bird.

ROOK
Corvus frugilegus

In the bare trees of a northern winter, the script is written by the network of stark, leafless twigs writing against the colour-drained sky, denuded by the ravages of autumn and with the green light of spring still far away. Here, though, on a warmer day, the heart can be lifted by the sight of rooks refurbishing their nests. Exceptionally early breeders, these loquacious colonial birds are responding to inner impulses governed by the increasing day-length from late December onwards. Their timetable is internally programmed, and despite the meagreness of the season, their stick-arranging proves the inevitability of what is coming.

Rooks and their rookeries can be spotted over much of Europe and Asia where fields and woods intermix.

25

CROWNED EAGLE

Stephanoaetus coronatus

Africa's crowned eagle is not the world's largest eagle – that's the harpy eagle of South America – but it is certainly among the most ferocious. It has unusually large talons, too, and this has earned it a very rare distinction: it is occasionally inclined to prey on humans.

There are several documented records of the crowned eagle attacking children; the skull of a child has been found in a nest. As the birds rarely, if ever, scavenge dead bodies, the child was probably killed as food for the young. On another occasion a severed human arm was found among a crowned eagle cache. And a seven-year-old boy was witnessed being attacked and badly injured by an eagle that was killed during the attempt.

GREAT SPOTTED WOODPECKER
Dendrocopos major

It's mid-January, and the forests of Europe and Asia resound, on fine days, to the atmospheric 'drumming' of the great spotted woodpecker. The sound is made by the bird striking wood with its bill ten or so times in less than a second.

The distinctive noise, though, is not the sound of a bird drilling a hole. It is purely for show, a replacement for the song of other birds, to advertise an individual's presence. It is like a drum roll, hitting a surface to make a sound, but not damaging it.

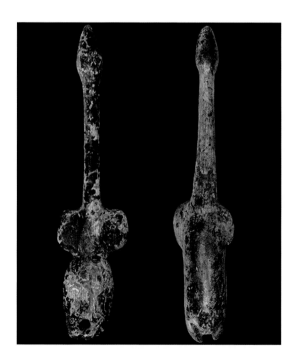

WHOOPER SWAN
Cygnus cygnus

Swans have enthralled humankind for millennia. That much is clear from artefacts found in Eastern Siberia, at a site called Mal'ta, near Irkutsk. Depicting birds with long necks and heavy bodies, they are carved from mammoth tusks and are thought to be 15,000 years old.

Imagine that: our ancestors would have heard the bugling calls of swans as they hunted the long-extinct mammoth.

SNOWY OWL
Bubo scandiacus

Although widespread, snowy owls are thinly scattered across the high latitudes of North America and Eurasia.

The big cat of the bird world, with its piercing yellow eyes, luxuriant plumage and brilliant white coloration, the snowy owl is one of the great symbols of the Arctic, together with polar bears and reindeer. In common with big cats, its looks bely its character, which can be extremely aggressive. Humans and other predators, such as wolves, have been attacked and injured by these great birds.

In common with several other Arctic predators, snowy owls depend largely on the tundra's production line of small mammals for food. They are particularly fond of lemmings – those supposedly suicidal rodents (it isn't true that they jump off cliffs) – and a single owl may consume around 1,600 of these a year.

Amazingly, some snowy owls remain in the Arctic all winter, even where the darkness does not relent. Here they often live near human settlements, using what light there is to hunt.

The largest member of the kingfisher family lives in open forests in eastern Australia and the far south-west.

LAUGHING KOOKABURRA
Dacelo novaeguineae

This Australian icon is part of the country's incredible dawn chorus. Well before it gets light, this chunky, brash bird will launch into its laughing call, and often the two members of a pair will sing in chorus. As a laugh, it is definitely on the hysterical end of the scale, becoming louder and more out of control as it goes on; a slapstick start to the day.

Those who are familiar with the Eurasian kingfisher – small, bejewelled and charming – are amazed when they hear that the kookaburra belongs to the same bird family. Hefty, plain-coloured, shunning rivers and impossible not to see – indeed, adorning powerlines, signposts, gum trees (of course!), fences and even barbecues – it is as far from the European perception of a kingfisher as it is possible to get.

It doesn't eat fish, either. It is a bird of dry country, with a voracious appetite for large insects, lizards, small mammals and occasionally snakes. The famously venomous spider fauna of Australia also takes a battering. The hunter simply sits on an elevated perch, scanning below, and slips down to snatch what it finds.

MARABOU STORK

Leptoptilos crumenifer

It's fair to say this is no one's favourite African bird. It is unattractive on a continent overflowing with colourful birds, it has revolting feeding habits and hangs out in insalubrious places such as rubbish tips, looking distinctly sinister.

This is a stork identifying as a vulture. It is a scavenger that occupies the fringes of vulture scrums, running in to pick up dropped scraps, or even mixing in at the carcass.

The marabou also, though, has a sideline in predation. At rubbish tips it eats rats and mice, which is very helpful to the human population. It also eats flamingos at their colonies, catching and drowning them, and then tearing them apart.

WHITE TERN
Gygis alba

An apparition from tropical seas sometimes called the angel tern, this pure white beauty with soothing dark eyes builds one of the most remarkable nests in the world – and that is no nest at all. It simply lays its single, speckled white egg precariously perched on a bare branch. No frills.

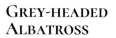

GREY-HEADED ALBATROSS
Thalassarche chrysostoma

After breeding, adult grey-headed albatrosses take a sabbatical to spend the next year wandering the oceans. Some simply set their wings to the wind and circumnavigate the globe, and some even do this twice! One radio-tracked individual from Bird Island, South Georgia, flew around the world in 46 days. That's an average of almost 600 miles (950km) per day.

These birds have also been tracked flying at over 80mph (130km/h) during a storm.

DOWNY WOODPECKER
Dryobates pubescens

A backyard bird over most of North America, the downy woodpecker is the pint-sized version of woodpeckerdom. It uses its diminutive stature to climb up weed stems as well as tree trunks, and to forage far out in the topmost, spindliest twigs of the canopy, foraging sites out of the reach of larger woodpeckers.

This bird demonstrates how, among birds, males and females may have significantly different ecological niches. Male downy woodpeckers almost always use the thinnest twigs and branches and consequently forage higher up and lower down (on snags and weeds) than females, which use trunks and branches with a greater diameter. When males are experimentally removed, the females will venture into the niches left behind.

Averaging only 15cm (6in) in length, this small woodpecker is common throughout most of North America in any wooded habitat; also gardens.

EMU
Dromaius novaehollandiae

This iconic flightless giant has been found throughout mainland Australia for millennia, as shown by this 2,000-year-old aboriginal depiction of emu feet found at Carnarvon Gorge, Queensland.

Today is Australia Day. The emu is the national bird of Australia and aptly so, for it has been part of the way of life of Aboriginal communities for many thousands of years. It has long been appreciated as a source of meat, and the fat has been used as a lubricant and as a dressing for wounds. Every part of the bird was used. The feathers were, not surprisingly, used as adornments in rituals, the eggs were eaten and the eggshells used as small carriers for water. The long leg bones were sometimes used for more gruesome purposes – as a spear to pierce the chest of an enemy who lay sleeping.

The Aboriginal peoples caught emus in many ways, none more ingenious than poisoning the tall, flightless birds' water supply. The hunters would crush the dry leaves of the pitchuri thornapple, a plant containing nicotine and nornicotine, and use the powder to contaminate small waterholes. The birds would drink, become stupefied, and were easy to kill.

SCARLET ROBIN
Petroica boodang

The eucalypt forests of south-east and extreme south-west Australia and Tasmania are the territories of this monogamous bird.

In the history of European settlement, it was common for people to give the animals and birds of their new land epithets that were familiar back home. It probably gave comfort to homesick people. Sometimes the result is a little incongruous, though. The New World warblers don't warble. And the American robin – well, it's not even a robin on steroids.

At times, though, the glove fits, and this is certainly the case for the delightful scarlet robin, of Australia. DNA studies show that it isn't at all closely related to a European robin, but in its habits it is remarkably similar, as well as bearing that smart scarlet breast. It is, for example, similarly a perch-and-pounce insectivore: both species perch above the ground on the lookout for small invertebrates, which they then swoop down to catch. Both are territorial. The similarity also extends to some of their breeding behaviour. The female builds the nest, for example, but the male provides her with food to keep her going, passed from bill to bill.

The similarities come from convergent evolution; the convergent naming came later.

WHITE-EYED RIVER MARTIN
Pseudochelidon sirintarae

Recorded in winter from a lake in Thailand, breeding grounds unknown. Probably extinct.

On the evening of 28 January 1968, a small bird flopped into a net at Bung Boraphet, an artificial lake in central Thailand. A swallow-like bird, it was taken to local zoologist Kitti Thonglongya, who immediately realised from its large white eyes and velvety plumage that it was something completely new to science. This was astonishing, bearing in mind that Thailand had been well explored by ornithologists for more than 100 years and Bueng Boraphet was nothing more exotic than a big lake (previously a swamp) in a large area of human population, the last place you might expect to find something new.

The following night another was captured, and on 10 February 1968, seven more. The next winter another appeared. A pair was delivered to Bangkok Zoo in 1971 and six were seen over the lake on 3 February 1978.

And that was it. The white-eyed river martin was never seen again. Where it came from and where it went is a complete mystery.

INDIAN VULTURE
Gyps indicus

Once abundant throughout India and Pakistan, the population has crashed, and is now very localised.

It wasn't long ago that the skies above India swirled with vultures, riding the plumes of warm air above the seething melting pot of humanity. Unloved, but usually unhindered, vultures and kites thrived in unsanitary corners, performing an astonishing clean-up service, relishing the ever-present reality of death and decay. Such was their efficiency and ubiquity that they inveigled their way into human culture, most notably that of the Parsis, a Persian minority concentrated in southern India.

Quite simply, the Parsis adopted the practice of letting the vultures dispose of their dead, a tradition known as 'sky burial'. After death, the human bodies would be taken up a moderately tall, fortified tower known as a *dakhma* (often colloquially called a Tower of Silence) where, after the funeral, they were exposed to the elements and to flesh-eating birds.

In the 1980s and 1990s, however, a catastrophe occurred when a drug called diclofenac began to be used as an anti-inflammatory for livestock. It proved toxic to vultures and the population crashed. From a population of 80 million in the 1980s, the numbers have sunk to a few thousand. The result is a crisis of sanitation. Other scavengers, including feral dogs, have vastly increased, while rates of infection have also soared. And, for the moment, the Parsis are having difficulty effectively disposing of their dead.

GURNEY'S PITTA
Hydrornis gurneyi

Vanishingly rare in one rainforest in Thailand and a few in Myanmar.

Pittas are probably the most beautiful birds in the world that you've never heard of. Found in the leaf litter of forests in tropical Asia, Australasia and Africa, they are secretive birds which, despite their gaudy plumage, are difficult to see in the half-light of the shade where they hunt. Each of the 30 or so species is breathtakingly colourful or boldly patterned. You would think that they would be among the best known of all birds, along with the similarly scintillant hummingbirds and birds-of-paradise.

Take a look at the Gurney's pitta. This bird, among the most beautiful of all, is on the verge of extinction. Can you imagine a world without it?

AMERICAN FLAMINGO
Phoenicopterus ruber

These flamingos take 2–3 years to gain their full hot-pink colour. They are localised around Caribbean, Central America and the Galapagos Islands, usually in salty lagoons.

Everyone knows flamingos: they are tall, pink and strange-looking. But in spite of this, everything about them makes sense. Flamingos have existed for 10 million years; their body plan works.

Take those long, bare legs. Flamingos often feed in hypersaline water, so it pays not to immerse too many feathers that might become encrusted with salt, or otherwise damaged. The birds need to be tall so that they can wade at different depths, and their necks must also be long enough to reach the water. Flamingos can also swim, using their webbed feet.

And what about the colour? It is certainly unusual but is simply the by-product of what the birds eat, which in the case of the American flamingo is crustaceans and algae rich in carotenoid pigments.

And what of their curious bill, oddly bent in the middle? Well, flamingos are filter feeders, and their bills are fitted above and below with tiny, comb-like structures called lamellae which together overlap and form a sieve from which small items in suspension can be trapped. The tongue is used as a piston to force water through the network of lamellae.

This filter system only works when the bill is slightly open. The advantage of the bent bill is that, when it is open, the space between mandibles remains the same from base to tip. If the bill was straight, the gap between the mandibles would be wider at the bill tip and very narrow at the base, making the filtration system less effective.

NORTHERN GANNET
Morus bassanus

With its 2m (6½ft) wingspan and gleaming, clean white plumage with crisp black wing-tips and butterscotch-infused crown, the northern gannet is an impressive seabird – and even more so when it plunge-dives into the sea to catch fish, sometimes from a considerable height, occasionally 30m (100ft). It hits the water head-first at speeds up to 95km/h (59mph), closing its wings at the last minute to maximize speed. To prevent damage, the gannet's nostrils open internally into the bill-chamber; otherwise the water would rush up its nose.

The dazzling plumage may help gannets to congregate easily at a food source. They can see one another from such a great distance that, if one begins plunge-diving, others far away will spot the action, and birds even further away will see their neighbours change course towards the commotion. The presence of many plunge-diving predators confuses and panics the shoals of fish, potentially making them easier to catch.

The northern gannet breeds on cliffs and islands of the North Atlantic and flies mainly over shelf waters.

LAKE DUCK
Oxyura vittata

This record-breaking duck can be found on freshwater lakes and wetlands in southern South America.

Birds don't exhibit much in the way of penises. On the whole, a coming together of reproductive organs is enough for fertilization to take place, with little or no intrusion required. However, there are certain situations where a penis, or more correctly a 'cloacal phallus', is highly necessary. Birds that copulate on unstable surfaces, such as water, need a little more purchase. Or, in the case of Argentina's lake duck, a lot of purchase. This species holds the record for the longest avian penis. At 42.5cm (16¾in), it is as long, or even longer than the bird itself, and longer than that of an ostrich (just 20cm/8in). The penis is spiral-shaped and can be retracted after use.

Why the lake duck is so richly endowed is not known.

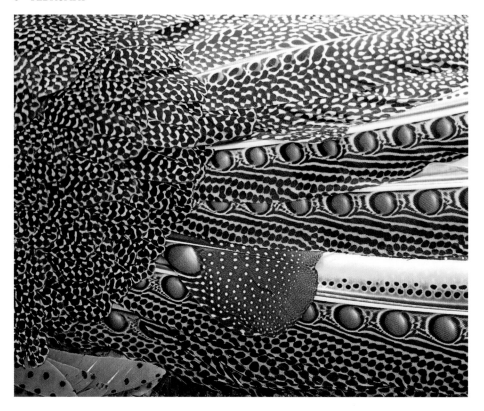

GREAT ARGUS
Argusianus argus

This pheasant
is native to the
dense forests
of the Malay
Peninsula,
Sumatra and
Borneo. Displays
are beginning
about now.

Argus was the hundred-eyed giant of ancient Greek mythology. He was charged by the goddess Hera with protecting the priestess Io, who had been transformed into a cow, the sort of thing that seemed to happen a lot in those days. Unfortunately, Argus was killed by Hermes, and thus failed in his mission. His eyes were thrown by Hera into the tail of a peacock. And, don't you know it, the peacock has overshadowed the argus ever since.

The great argus occurs in warmer tropical regions than the peacock, in south-east Asia, usually in thick forest. Its call is a purer, less clanging effort, sounding like an impressed 'Oh, wow!' Its display is similar, with the tail coverts fanned almost all around the face and body, but its many eye spots are not as large or ornate. Nonetheless, without the brilliance of the peacock, the great argus, bearing some of the longest feathers in the whole bird world, would probably be just as famous and renowned.

RED JUNGLEFOWL (DOMESTIC CHICKEN)
Gallus gallus

Distributed worldwide in captivity, in the wild it is found in woodland in India and south-east Asia.

Today is as good as any day to celebrate the domestic chicken, the world's most widely eaten bird. Fifty billion are reared annually as a source of meat and eggs. However, on this day in 1975, the population of the city of Haicheng, China, would find themselves grateful to chickens. On 4 February a magnitude 7.5 earthquake struck the city and 2,000 people were killed. However, in the preceding weeks the locals had observed a great deal of strange behaviour among animals. Chickens would run around their coops in panic in the middle of the night and had stopped laying eggs. Cows and horses were restless. Even snakes left their hibernation hideouts and many froze to death. The behaviour was so unusual that the Chinese authorities, who had also noticed odd groundwater events and seismic foreshocks, decided to evacuate the city about 12 hours before the earthquake struck. It is estimated that 150,000 lives were saved following what has been the only successful earthquake prediction in history.

COMMON HAWK-CUCKOO
Hierococcyx varius

Around now, the 'brain-fever bird' is just beginning to sing in woodlands from Pakistan to India, Bagladesh and south to Sri Lanka.

Almost everyone on the Indian subcontinent knows the common hawk-cuckoo, but not by that name. They know it as the notorious 'brain-fever bird', or perhaps just as the bird that could conceivably have the most annoying call in the world. It isn't that the three-note advertisement is inherently untuneful, it is that it is repeated in short cycles, each three-note rendition slightly rising in pitch and sounding, as it continues, concerned, worried, alarmed, desperate, delirious. The sense of anxiety in the rising pitch is palpable.

The bird doesn't help by calling endlessly, from well before dawn to late dusk, and all through the day. There is no escape from the rising sense of panic – and all this in the pre-monsoon heat, too. A brain-fever indeed.

SOUTHERN BROWN KIWI
Apteryx australis

Secretive, nocturnal flightless emblem of New Zealand forests.

It is Waitangi Day, the national day of New Zealand, and the country's national bird is a real oddity. Apart from the penguins, it must rank as the least bird-like of birds, the complete outlier. The five species of kiwis have only rudimentary wings, and their feathers are fine and hair-like. The Kiwi lays an egg that is 25 per cent of its body weight, by far the largest ratio of any bird.

Kiwis are shy, nocturnal creatures with long, slightly down-curved bills. Uniquely among birds (again) its nostrils are set at the tip of the bill. The olfactory (smelling) part of a kiwi's brain is ten times larger than any other bird, and it spends the hours of darkness probing in the soil and leaf litter to find worms and other invertebrates. Another odd habit is that, as it forages, the kiwi sniffs constantly. This happens because, as soon as it detects food, the nasal gland releases mucus. The nasal openings are small and slit-like, and become clogged easily, hence the incessant sniffling.

STELLER'S SEA EAGLE
Haliaeetus pelagicus

Above: This eagle breeds on coasts of north-east Asia and winters south to Japan and the Korean Peninsula.

Top right: This tiny bird is only found in northern Peru.

Bottom right: The Australian 'peewee' (also found in parts of New Guinea and Timor) can't stand his own reflection.

A single Steller's sea eagle is an impressive sight, with its enormous yellow bill, sturdy body and broad, brown and white wings. It is the world's heaviest bird of prey. So, imagine seeing a large group. This is what happens every February on Japan's Nemuro Straits, off the island of Hokkaido. Forced south by pack ice, around 1,000 birds gather in an area near the town of Rausu to feed on abundant Pacific cod, which they catch by plunging, talons-first, into the water. There is a local fishing industry here, too, which also provides a source of food for the eagles, and tourist boats go out to watch the birds and attract them by throwing out fish. Seeing a plunging eagle close-up is a sight to remember.

MARVELLOUS SPATULETAIL
Loddigesia mirabilis

This hummingbird takes outrageous, ornate adornments to the limit. It stretches our credulity to the limit, too, but it really exists.

It's the only bird in the world with just four tail feathers, each of which it can move independently. When displaying, the ping pong ball-sized male flies backwards and forwards over a branch in an arc, creating a very strange effect as its spatules appear to wobble in all directions. The females are duly mesmerized.

MAGPIE-LARK
Grallina cyanoleuca

One of the most familiar birds of Australia, the magpie-lark is found in almost every corner of the continent, except Tasmania, from sheep country to suburban lawn. Its loud call, often given by pairs in duet, has earned it the near-universal nickname 'pewee'.

Magpie-larks are notorious for their extreme territorial behaviour, frequently attacking people and animals. They are also legendary for launching themselves at their own reflections, with great vigour.

COMMON BLACKBIRD
Turdus merula

The national bird of Sweden lives in woodland, scrub and the gardens of Europe as well as parts of the Middle East.

It's February, and the woods and suburbs of Europe are beginning to resound with the songs of blackbirds, who add poise and class to the chorus with their fluty, unhurried songs. They are the last resident bird to begin in earnest, and their song is surely the loveliest.

Blackbirds weren't always cherished, as this English nursery rhyme attests:

Sing a song of sixpence, a pocketful of rye;
Four and twenty blackbirds baked in a pie.
When the pie was opened, the birds began to sing;
Wasn't that a dainty dish to set before the King?

At first this may not make sense, but it was a tradition in Medieval England to put live birds and animals into a pie after it was cooked, so that once the crust was opened the unfortunate creatures would erupt from the pie to provide entertainment for the guests.

ROCK PTARMIGAN
Lagopus muta

Found in extreme tundra and high mountains across Eurasia and North America, this member of the grouse family is known as *raichō* in Japan – 'thunder bird'.

Of all the world's birds, the ptarmigan is probably the hardiest. It is the only species that never retreats from the tundra, either on mountains or in the Arctic. However cold you might be, the ptarmigan will be somewhere chillier. Its range reaches deep into the Arctic Circle, even in winter, and it breeds as far north as any other bird.

It has a number of adaptations to assist in its extreme lifestyle. Its feet are densely and permanently feathered, not just to reduce heat loss from bare areas, but also to help the bird walk in the snow – the feathering increases the foot surface area by a factor of four and makes excellent snow shoes. The rest of the feathers are fluffy at the base (fluffier in winter) to give more effective insulation. In extreme conditions birds will dig snow holes for shelter. They are also somewhat sluggish and eat a vegetarian diet, which is nutritious but doesn't raise their metabolic rate unduly high.

12TH FEBRUARY

EGYPTIAN VULTURE

Neophron percnopterus

If you like delightful, inspiring, feel-good stories about birds, wait until tomorrow.

The Egyptian vulture relishes a very unusual dietary item – excrement. This includes human faeces, which the vulture eats at rubbish tips and other suitable locations. It eats many other types, too, and it is thought that the poo of large, herbivorous animals may provide the birds with carotenoid pigments. These make vulture's face yellow, and ironically, given their source, are an indication of its health and fitness.

13TH FEBRUARY

LUZON BLEEDING-HEART

Gallicolumba luzonica

It is almost St Valentine's Day, so you're unlucky in love, take some comfort in the knowledge that birds can suffer from broken hearts too – or at least, bleeding hearts. Many people think that pigeons are boring, but anyone setting eyes on the gorgeous Luzon bleeding-heart will soon change their mind. There are five species of bleeding-heart pigeons, all of them found only in the Philippines. All are rare and three species are classified as critically endangered on the International Union for Conservation of Nature's Red List.

SUPERB FAIRYWREN
Malurus cyaneus

Above: The
Australian male
fairywren brings
gifts of yellow
petals as tokens
of seduction.

Top left: African
'pharoah's chickens'
can be seen in
Spain as well as
Asia and India.

Bottom left: Found
in the forests of
Luzon, Philippines.

Throughout much of the world, today is St Valentine's Day, a festival devoted to the celebration of romantic love. Many millions of lovers will exchange gifts and cards and, most commonly, flowers.

Amazingly, there are also some birds in the world that give their lover flowers – or, at least, flower petals. These are the fairywrens of Australia. On certain mornings in the pre-breeding season (usually October), males visit their prospective mate before dawn, while it is still dark, and sometimes bring petals for courting purposes.

There is, though, shade to this sunlight. Fairywrens are famous for their profligacy outside the pair-bond; they routinely visit neighbouring females for sex that are officially paired to other males. And it is to these 'mistresses' that their floral gifts are given.

BLUE TIT
Cyanistes caeruleus

An abundant woodland bird in much of Europe, south-east to Iran.

All over Europe, blue tits are in full song, uttering their cheerful trills from the still-bare treetops. They say that every resident bird should be paired by St Valentine's Day (14 February) and there is much truth to this. If a male bird hasn't already attracted a mate with his song, he is by now well behind.

It is often said that all the colourful birds are in the tropics, but the sublimely showy blue tit, all yellow and blue, is one of many exceptions, although it is so common in Europe that its delights are often overlooked.

In recent years, scientists have discovered that there is more to the blue tit's stunning colours than meets the eye – literally. The blue parts of the plumage simply glow with ultraviolet reflectance, and the birds often use this to assess each other's suitability as a mate.

HARPY EAGLE
Harpia harpyja

The strongest, mightiest eagle in the Americas also possesses the largest talons, capable of grabbing monkeys from the treetops. It is a totemic species of undisturbed tall tropical rainforest, placing its huge, bulky nest high in a forest giant. It is the ultimate apex predator, ferocious and magnificent. It is also thinly distributed, rare and seldom seen.

Capable of carrying off an animal 6kg (13lb) in weight, its most frequent food item is sloths, but monkeys are also favoured, and other mammals such as porcupines, kinkajous and agoutis may also be taken. The harpy eagle hunts by watching from a canopy perch for nearby prey and making a quick ambush when something is spotted.

NORTHERN PINTAIL
Anas acuta

The distinctive pintail breeds on lakes across the northern half of Eurasia and North America; winters to the south, to West Africa and in India.

Wild ducks in winter are an arresting sight, and no more so than the handsome pintail, the males with chocolate-brown heads and butter-coloured bottoms, not to mention the intricate stripes and patterns of delicate grey, as neat as latticework. The females are a greyish-brown all their own and both sexes have a regal mien, peering upon the world from their long necks.

Now, in February, the winter flocks of pintails have reached fever-pitch in fidgetiness. Birds shake their heads, stretch their necks, waggle their bottoms, chase, splash and many times simply take off from the water on a long circular flight – female leading, several males in tow. It might be early, but it's the display season and nobody hides in a corner.

CRIMSON SUNBIRD
Aethopyga siparaja

This 11cm (4¼in) bird is widespread in gardens and forest edge from India, China and south-east Asia to Indonesia and Sulawesi.

At this time of year, the crimson sunbirds are starting to breed in Singapore, where they are the unofficial national bird. Tiny, brilliantly coloured and much at home in flower-encrusted gardens, they are rightly cherished. The sunbirds are an equivalent family to hummingbirds in the Old World, and they rival those remarkable birds in being the principal nectar-drinkers of their region (Asia and Africa). They also rival them in sheer stunning beauty. They rarely hover, but instead perch while drinking. The crimson sunbird of south-east Asia often pierces the base of long blooms to 'steal' the nectar. In addition to nectar, it is also a scourge on the local spider population.

In common with other sunbirds, this bird builds a delightful, purse-shaped nest, often in garden shrubs. It is delicate and fine, but the builders deliberately place all manner of useless objects on its edge to disguise what it actually is – things like string, cobwebs or incongruous pieces of bark.

COMMON CHAFFINCH
Fringilla coelebs

Very common in woodland and gardens from Europe east to Central Asia and south to North Africa, Atlantic islands, the chaffinch sings in his regional dialect.

Many birds resident in Europe begin singing as soon as the days start to get longer, but the chaffinch holds off, and doesn't get going properly until February. The song is a cheerful ditty endlessly repeated; a trill that accelerates to a flourish to finish. It has been likened to the action of a slow bowler in cricket, accelerating to the crease and then quickly releasing the ball – which is fine, so long as you understand the sport.

If these birds are around you, listen carefully around now and you will hear something odd – not full songs, but halting, rather half-hearted attempts at the phrase. These are made by yearlings practising the song. They will have got the general idea from their father and neighbours but now, in pre-season, they begin to try out their own songs. At first their efforts are amateurish and changeable – they are known as 'plastic songs' – but will soon mature into the real thing. It's a case of single-use plastic song.

NORTHERN LAPWING
Vanellus vanellus

A wader that is a common breeder on arable land across much of Europe and Asia, some wintering further south.

It doesn't matter how cold it is, or how much the late winter bites, lapwings return to their territories at this time of year, come what may. Catch a sunny morning and they will show you how the sap of spring is rising, even as it still seems to lie hidden and inert. The lapwing takes to the air with swoops and whoops, performing circles and figures of eight above its territory, turning this way and that, throwing its body from side to side, almost out of control, all the time making wild, ecstatic cries. It is drunk on spring.

WHOOPING CRANE
Grus americana

Breeding on Canadian wetlands the whooping crane winters on saltmarshes on Texas coast – in 2018 the crane population in Aransas topped the 500 mark.

About now a very special event is taking place in Port Aransas, south Texas, USA: the annual Whooping Crane Festival. The fact that it runs at all is a stunning conservation success story.

The whooping crane was once arguably the world's rarest bird. In 1938 the whole population comprised just 15 adults. A familiar woeful tale of shooting and habitat destruction was the culprit. However, a campaign of public education, general concern for America's tallest bird and the protection of the bird's breeding habitat at Wood Buffalo National Park, in Canada, and Aransas National Wildlife Refuge, all helped to stabilize the population. Nevertheless, until quite recently the numbers increased at an achingly slow pace.

In the 2000s, it was decided that a second population should be established, away from the wild migratory flock, as an insurance against disaster striking the remaining birds. The International Crane Foundation decided to establish a captive breeding population in Wisconsin, but in order for these birds to be reintroduced into the wild, they needed a wintering site. Florida was selected, but how would the birds find their way there? An audacious plan led to young cranes being reared in captivity, fed and looked after by people clad in crane costumes, and then conditioned to follow microlight aircraft to their new wintering site. Amazingly, teaching the birds to fly to a wintering site proved successful, although so far, no self-sustaining wild population has been established. Hopefully, to reward such amazing efforts, it will do so in the near future.

HOATZIN
Opisthocomus hoazin

I s there a stranger bird in the whole world than the hoatzin of Amazonian waterways? With its bizarre, wispy crest, staring red eye, ridiculously small head and bulky body, it resembles a feathered dinosaur that escaped the mass extinction around 65 million years ago (which, incidentally, is exactly what birds are).

A strange feature of hoatzin biology recalls a dinosaur even more: nestlings have two claws on the digits of their wings. When threatened in the nest, which is sited above water, the young hoatzins evacuate the platform and jump on to the branches below, using their claws to scramble around. If the threat is extreme, the chicks dive into the water and can swim under the surface to escape. Once the danger passes, the claws are employed to clamber up the branches and into the nest again.

This colourful leaf-eater breeds in rainy season in sheltered waterways in Amazonia which, in much of its range, is about now.

GREAT FRIGATEBIRD
Fregata minor

Male and female frigate birds have a red gular sac at the neck. The male forces air into his to inflate it like a balloon and thereby attract a mate. They are found mainly in the tropical Indian and Pacific oceans, breeding on islands at any time of year.

Frigatebirds are dark, marauding sea birds with long, pointed wings and forked tails, fancifully recalling the long-extinct pterosaurs. They have the largest wing area relative to body weight of any bird in the world, which makes them the global expert at generating lift. This is just as well, because frigatebirds wander for vast distances over the open ocean, without the convenience of having waterproof feathers – something that is highly unusual for sea birds. Landing on the water would be fatal!

Research on great frigatebirds shows that, even when breeding on the Galapagos Islands they often fly without stopping for ten or more days at a time. During this period, they only sleep for short bursts, a total of 48 minutes out of 24 hours. On land they manage 12 hours out of every 24, usually with only one side on the brain 'asleep' and the other alert. Sleep patterns in birds are very strange indeed!

Above: The persistent northern goshawk, found in forests of Eurasia, North America and northern Central America.

Top right: This robin lives in all kinds of forests and gardens throughout North America; resident south of Great Lakes.

Bottom right: Common throughout most of Africa in bush and scrub.

NORTHERN GOSHAWK

Accipiter gentilis

F ew raptors are more widely admired by falconers than the formidable goshawk, a fast and powerful bird of prey adapted to hunting in forests. It sits silently on a perch for about 10 minutes at a time, watching for the movement of prey in the vicinity. If nothing happens, it will switch perch. Once it has spotted something, it manoeuvres carefully into position to make a surprise lunge, and then accelerates rapidly on approach. Once it has sunk its claws into the flesh of prey, death comes quickly. The meal may be a bird, ranging from pigeon to grouse, or a mammal, such as a hare.

What so captures the imagination of admirers is the goshawk's sheer recklessness in the hunt. Once it has locked onto prey, it will readily smash through the undergrowth to reach it, or even enter the water; at times it will chase grounded prey by running. It has been known to pursue a single hare for an hour and a squirrel for 15 minutes – pure, ruthless drive and aggression.

AMERICAN ROBIN
Turdus migratorius

The robin is one of the most widespread and familiar birds in North America, occurring everywhere from urban gardens to remote woodland. At this time of the year, its high-pitched, liquid song, carefully phrased, is just beginning to cut through the cold air, a sure sign of spring to come.

The robin is one of the very first birds to sing on a spring day, starting well before the rest of the dawn chorus when it is still truly dark – sometimes 3am. It sings alone again in the deep twilight.

HELMETED GUINEAFOWL
Numida meleagris

Speed-dating isn't a human invention. Helmeted guineafowl did it first. In the early part of the breeding season, males chase each other. After a couple of weeks, the best males emerge from the pack. Then the males chase the females. In a curious mirror of current (Western) human behaviour, there then follows a period in which guineafowl relationships form and then split, form again and split again. The speed-dating ends as abruptly as it starts, and then the birds form stable pairs.

IVORY-BILLED WOODPECKER
Campephilus principalis

The ivory-billed woodpecker is probably extinct but hope remains that is could still inhabite the extensive old-growth forests and swamps of south-eastern USA and Cuba.

The huge Ivory-billed woodpecker once ranged across large parts of the south-eastern United States, from Florida in the east, west to Texas and north to Arkansas, as well as on the island of Cuba. It inhabited large, old-growth forests with an abundance of large beetles, typically remote and far away from human habitation. Whether it still exists is a matter of mystery, mayhem, perhaps some mischief, and a great deal of muddle.

What is beyond doubt is that many years ago it declined towards extinction. The last irrefutable record in the USA was in April 1944, and in Cuba it probably hung on until the 1990s. Since then, some hope has always persisted that it might still exist somewhere remote. There were occasional reports and sightings, but never with significant corroborative evidence.

Then, on 27 February 2004, two highly respected ornithologists, Tim Gallagher and Bobby Harrison, were following a tip-off in eastern Arkansas when a large black-and-white woodpecker flew past them. Mayhem ensued. Based on its wing pattern the two men were convinced they had seen an ivory-billed woodpecker. Many people believed them, to the extent that a massive search operation was launched in the area. Over the next few years sightings were reported, birds were supposedly heard 'drumming', and a video was captured. At about the same time ivory-bills were reported in Florida, once again with multiple sightings. Scientific papers announcing the rediscoveries were published.

The problem was that the combined searches yielded not a shred of irrefutable evidence. The bird in the video was dismissed by some as the closely related pileated woodpecker (*Dryocopus pileatus*). Crucially, no photographs or videos of the distinctive bird's specific field marks were ever made, and no feathers or other body parts were found.

The incident caused massive controversy and divided North American birders into two camps, believers and non-believers. It continues to do so.

ROSY-FACED LOVEBIRD
Agapornis roseicollis

Popular as a cage bird, this charmer's natural habitat is woodland and semi-desert in extreme south-west Africa.

The lovebirds are a group of tiny parrots that live in Africa. Their English common and scientific names come from the strength of a couple's pair bond, which is demonstrated by the habit of nuzzling up together and preening each other in a public show of affection worthy of any tabloid exclusive.

Their neat, cup-shaped nest, usually built in a crevice, is unusual among parrots. For a family that doesn't generally bother with a nest at all, that's a big deal. An even bigger surprise, though, and this is possibly unique among all birds, is the way in which the female carries material to the nest site. In contrast to all other birds, who simply hold it in their bills, the rosy-faced lovebird tucks the items into her plumage, usually around the rump area, and carries it like that.

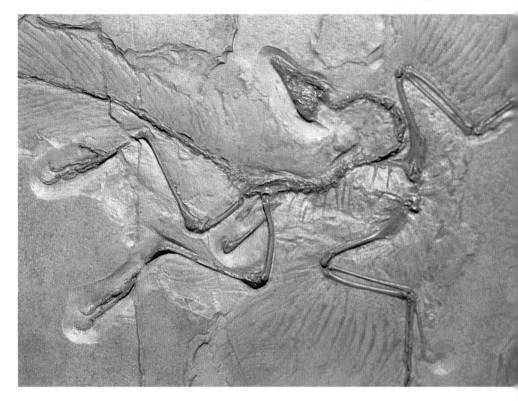

ARCHAEOPTERYX
Archaeopteryx lithographica

About the size of a Eurasian magpie, the archaeopteryx was a glider that inhabited the warm, tropical swamps of what is now Germany 150 million years ago.

It's leap-year day, so here's something a little different – the world's most famous fossil bird, which has been extinct for about 150 million years.

The bones of *Archaeopteryx* were first discovered in 1861, near Langenaltheim, Germany, just two years after Darwin published his seminal book *On the Origin of Species*. It immediately attracted worldwide fame as a 'missing link' between birds and reptiles, since it showed characteristics of both. Its avian features include a wishbone, wings and, of course, feathers. Its non-avian features include teeth and a bony tail. It is a compelling mixture.

These days the difference between birds and reptiles, especially dinosaurs, has blurred. Effectively, birds are now known to be the only dinosaur strand that survived the mass extinction 65 million years ago.

The Late Jurassic *Archaeopteryx* could still be the first bird, but whether it is a bird or a bird-like dinosaur is still disputed. Even now, 160 years on, it still causes controversy.

HOUSE SPARROW
Passer domesticus

Native to
Eurasia, Europe
east to India
and Myanmar.
Introduced
worldwide.
Males may well
be fighting now –
this one looks like
it has been.

Today, take a look at your sparrows. The chances are that there will be some nearby, as the house sparrow is one of the world's most common and ubiquitous species, occurring wherever we do – even in city centres and down mines. Everybody takes the sparrow for granted, and few people ever actually look at them in detail.

But for a moment, enjoy the plain-coloured females, with their streak of pale eyeshadow. Look at the males, too, with their black throat and chest band. Scientists have shown that the extent of black is a direct reflection of a male's dominance in its social group, the blacker the better. The size of badge is a true reflection of a bird's quality; the birds with the largest black patches have the best fighting ability.

MANDARIN DUCK
Aix galericulata

Breeds in north-east Asia, migrates south to southern China; resident of Japan. Introduced in Britain and parts of Europe.

A bird to brighten dark days, possibly like today, the mandarin duck is an example of just how colourful and showy ducks (or at least drakes) can be. Males genuinely do make a habit of displaying on gloomy, cloudy days; the birds have large eyes and see well at low light levels. They often feed on the forest floor of deciduous woodlands, picking up acorns and other fruits. Oddly, the mandarin duck nests in tree holes, often high above the ground, and in east Asia the species relies on the Black Woodpecker to excavate them.

The remarkable orange 'sails' on the male's back are modified secondary flight feathers. Not surprisingly, they are shown off to advantage in display – an effective 'sails' pitch.

NORTHERN WHEATEAR
Oenanthe oenanthe

This insectivore tends to hop or run about on the ground. It breeds across northern Eurasia, Greenland and Alaska in tundra and open habitats. Migrates to Africa south of the Sahara.

An enthusiast at trying its luck, the super-migratory wheatear is always one of the first summer visitors to arrive back at its breeding grounds – in temperate Europe by March – and one of the last to leave, with hangers-on staying well into November. Finally, though, all members of the population retreat to tropical Africa for the depths of winter.

The last fact is remarkable, because northern wheatears breed all across Eurasia. In the west they spill over to Greenland, and in the east they extend so far across northern Asia that some breed in Alaska. Yet birds from both extremities join the family in Africa in winter. From a far-flung location this can involve a one-way journey of 15,000km (over 9,300 miles) and, for birds migrating from Greenland, substantial ocean crossings.

Logic would dictate that a bird breeding in Alaska or Greenland might migrate due south to reach milder climes in Central America, and those breeding in Siberia should just hop south to India. But they don't. It is thought that this shows the evolution of their migration. Towards the end of the last ice age, 11,700 years ago, the ice retreated slowly, and each decade or so it would become more and more hospitable in the north, with greater areas of tundra becoming available. As the ice retreated so the wheatears advanced, but as their advance was so slow, their migratory routes increased only in small increments. The birds colonizing east and west never 'noticed' how much longer their routes were and they never changed them.

TREE SWALLOW
Tachycineta bicolor

This bird breeds right across North America from the Arctic southwards, usually near water. Winters mainly in Florida and around the Gulf of Mexico.

One swallow may not make a spring, but what about late winter? The tree swallow, with its soft, snow-white underparts, clean enough to feature in a washing-powder commercial, is the hardiest swallow in North America by far. It arrives in the south as early as January, and may even reach Canada in March, much earlier than its relatives.

The reason it can do this is down to a highly unusual dietary quirk. Although primarily adapted for catching flying insects, the tree swallow can, in times of emergency, become vegetarian. The mainstay is bayberries, the fruits of the wax myrtle, which very few other birds can digest. In the winter, tree swallows can subsist on bayberries for many days at a time.

COAL TIT
Periparus ater

Only 11.5cm (4½in) long, this bird favours conifer woods and can be found from Europe and North Africa east to the Himalayas, China and Japan.

Among bird-loving gardeners, the coal tit is best-known for being the fall guy in disputes with larger birds, the latter using their size to threaten and displace the coal tit from the feeder. It scuttles away, bullied by both great tits and blue tits, as well as other birds.

Among scientists, however, the coal tit is known for something quite different – its sex life. Intense sperm competition among males ensures that a high proportion of eggs in nests have not been fertilized by the father attending the nest but are by-products of extra-pair liaisons. The proportion, 25 per cent, is one of the highest for any bird in the world.

Amazingly – and here's a thought for the day – different populations of coal tit males have different lengths of spermatozoa. For example, in a long-term study coal tits in a Norwegian wood had longer sperm than those in a German wood!

CETTI'S WARBLER
Cettia cetti

Every classical music lover knows the spellbinding, crashing start to Edvard Grieg's piano concerto. It is one of the great openings of any piano piece.

Every birder knows the spellbinding, shouting, crashing start to the song of the Cetti's warbler. Hearing it close up is almost painful.

The two are similar in tone and form, almost suspiciously so.

Could Edvard Grieg have subconsciously drawn upon the loud song of the Cetti's warbler?

WALLCREEPER
Tichodroma muraria

Bursting with charisma, enflamed with wings of shining crimson, and viewed against a precipitous mountain backdrop, the wallcreeper has long been a birders' favourite. Its crisp beauty, with clean white spots on its black wing-tips, and the body of thunder-cloud grey, is alluring enough. Yet it also has a singular mien, flicking those wings as if seized with a nervous tic, and flying with extravagant, butterfly-like wingbeats and glides. If joy could be expressed in a single bird, the wallcreeper would be that bird.

EURASIAN DOTTEREL
Charadrius morinellus

Dotterels live a life that many a woman might have dreamt about. Hence the dotterel is a good symbol of International Women's Day.

In the breeding behaviour of this bird, the roles are reversed. The females are larger and much more colourful than the males. They are the ones that initiate courtship and display. Once they have laid eggs, female dotterels then usually abandon their clutch, leaving all the incubation, brooding and other family duties to the male. They might even leave the area after laying a clutch and metaphorically spend the rest of the summer at the spa.

Some females lay two clutches, one after the other, each with a different male, in what is known as serial polyandry.

And, just to show that they are cover all the bases, they will sometimes share incubation.

COMMON PHEASANT
Phasianus colchicus

Native to central and eastern Asia, the pheasant was introduced to Western Europe and North America.

There are few birds in the world shot at more frequently than the unfortunate pheasant. A native of Asia, even as far west as Greece, it is a showy gamebird with a legendary taste. As such it has played a part in human culture for millennia. The Romans considered it a great delicacy, and through medieval times up until the 19th century it was a rare and scarce treat. In 1823 about one-third of Britain's prison population was made up of poachers.

Today you can buy pheasant in your local supermarket, but in much of Europe (especially in the UK) and North America there is still an enormous industry devoted to shooting your own.

The bird itself, one forgets, is stunningly beautiful. The female largely ignores the male's feathered bling, and is far more interested in the small blue wattles on his red face.

MOURNING DOVE
Zenaida macroura

This dove commonly nests in trees in much of North America and into Mexico, often in suburbs. In the Rockies it is mainly a summer visitor.

The mourning dove is one of the most common birds in North America, with an estimated population of 350 million pairs in the USA alone. However, it is perhaps surprising that the continent isn't knee-deep in them, so much are they adapted for high productivity.

The breeding season usually begins in February and ends in October, but in the South it might carry on all year. A pair in Texas was recorded raising six consecutive broods, all of which, in classic pigeon style, consisted of two eggs.

The mourning dove is geared up so much for fast breeding that it will sometimes lay the next clutch only 30 days after the previous one, meaning that the squabs from one brood may not have left the nest by the time the next eggs arrive. The arrangement must get uncomfortable, to say the least.

WHITE STORK
Ciconia ciconia

Migrates in summer to parts of Europe, North Africa and western Asia; winters in sub-Saharan Africa and India.

People in many parts of Europe will have their eyes peeled around now, looking for the first migrant arrivals of white storks. Few birds anywhere will be more welcome, and few carry such symbolism.

Being a large, unmistakable white bird that often makes its voluminous stick nests on rooftops or on specially erected poles in villages, this stork isn't a migrant that you can miss. For thousands of years storks have been associated with good luck. They certainly provide a good service as they are voracious hunters of many of humankind's 'pests', such as mice and rats, large insects and small snakes.

One of many recurring legends, especially in Slavic and Germanic countries, is of the white stork as a bringer of babies. For example, if you were trying for a baby, it was wise to leave an edible gift for your local birds. The next spring, the storks would go to special caves, the home of the unborn, to collect the much-wanted child, carry it in a basket on its back or in its bill, and deliver it to the favoured household. This legend has persisted for many centuries; the bond between bird and people is a cherished one.

REED BUNTING
Emberiza schoeniclus

Resident over much of temperate Europe and Asia; many migrate in winter, for example to North Africa and northern India.

It's March and Eurasia's handsome male reed bunting is getting into his singing stride. He performs a disjointed, tuneless refrain, which could be likened to the halting efforts of a young child counting to three and forgetting what follows.

Intriguingly, though, there are two very obviously different songs. In one, the syllables have a steady pace, there are no more than three or four, and the gaps between songs are short. In the other, the notes are rushed, more are packed into the same length of phrase, but the gaps between them are longer.

Bear with this technical stuff, because it's fascinating – the steady song is sung by a paired bird and the rushed song by an unpaired bird. So, the reed bunting community – and listening birders – can tell an individual's breeding status just by tuning in.

WOODLARK
Lullula arborea

I n Europe, the skylark gets all the headlines and most of the love. As is so often the case, however, to aficionados the less celebrated bird is the best performer and worthy of greater admiration. So it is in the case of the woodlark. It is hard to convey the lilting, subtle cadence of the song of the woodlark, delivered from high in the air, where the bird circles for minutes on end. The phrase works down the semi-tones with ineffable softness, and accelerates with the pace of a small child going down a slide.

People have long sought to convey the song's loveliness. The scientific name *Lullula* is onomatopoeic, so is the French *Alouette lulu*. But perhaps Robbie Burns says it best in his poem 'Address to the Woodlark':

Oh, stay sweet warbling woodlark, stay
Nor quit for me the trembling spray;
A hapless lover courts thy lay,
Thy soothing, fond complaining.

Resident on woodland edge and scrub throughout Europe and east to Ukraine and Iraq; mainly a summer visitor in eastern Europe, Russsia and Turkey.

BLACK-AND-WHITE WARBLER
Mniotilta varia

Now is the time to look out for the first wood warbler of spring, which, in many parts of eastern North America, is the delightful black-and-white warbler, a stripy species that lives up to its name. It has the unusual habit of creeping up branches searching the bark, in the manner of a woodpecker or nuthatch, and is less dependent on the spring leaf-burst than other wood warblers. You cannot mistake its persistent 'weesa-weesa-weesa ...' song.

EASTERN PHOEBE
Sayornis phoebe

A soberly coloured, quiet and unobtrusive bird, the eastern phoebe has nonetheless found its way into the affections of many North American bird enthusiasts. This is for two reasons. First, its gentle 'fee-bee' song is one of the first migrant bird songs to be heard in the spring, often in March, a sure sign of the arrival of warmer weather. Second, it has the endearing habit of nesting in human artefacts, especially bridges, culverts and outbuildings.

EURASIAN WOODCOCK
Scolopax rusticola

Above: The woodcock breeds from Europe east across Asia to Japan.

Top left: Sensibly, this warbler winters in Central and northern South America.

Bottom left: This flycatcher is found in northern and eastern North America; it winters in the Gulf of Mexico north to the Carolinas.

Today, try to imagine that you are a woodcock. The woodcock is a type of shorebird, but it lives in woodland and primarily eats earthworms taken from the woodland floor.

First, try to look through its eyes, which are placed high on the sides of its head. This allows the woodcock panoramic vision, the ability to see all around, a trick that is useful for spotting danger. The woodcock also has some binocular vision, an arc where the eyes cover the same point simultaneously but from different sides of the head. Human eyes face forwards and overlap considerably, which gives us excellent binocular vision that helps us to judge distances.

But consider this. The woodcock has binocular vision immediately in front of it AND behind it. It can see front and back at the same time ... as well as all around.

Is that making you dizzy?

JAPANESE WHITE-EYE
Zosterops japonicus

The Japanese white-eye weighs just 11g (¼oz). You can find it in Japan, Korea, Philippines, Indonesia in all kinds of woodland; introduced Hawaii and other islands.

Have you ever wondered which birds you might see should you ever visit the world-famous cherry-blossom trees of Japan, the *sakura*? One answer is the diminutive Japanese white-eye, a common bird of eastern Asia which searches the blossoms for insects, but also eats fruit.

It is a highly adaptable species, as was shown in 1953 when it was introduced into the Hawaiian Islands, the isolated Pacific archipelago with a varied tropical climate. It immediately took a liking to the place and within a few years, remarkably, became the most common forest bird. There are now over a million individuals.

However, we know that ultimately the Hawaiian birds will become a separate species. Phylogenetic tests have shown that the 80 or so species of white-eyes are just about the fastest evolving birds in the world. So expect the next species in about 500,000 years.

LESSER HONEYGUIDE
Indicator minor

Found in wooded areas of Africa south of the Sahara, excluding tropical forest belt. Shown being chased off by two black-collared barbets (*Lybius torquatus*).

It doesn't look much, but this is one of the most peculiar birds in the world. The honeyguides are outriders in all kinds of ways. They are among the few birds in the world that eat beeswax, although they also forage for insects. They join the cuckoos in being brood parasites, always laying their eggs in the nests of other birds and subcontracting the parenting skills of the host. Their third unusual piece of behaviour is one of the most sinister traits found in any bird.

They lay a single egg in the nest of a host. When the youngster hatches, for a short time it has an extra piece on the top of its bill that makes it hook-shaped. The young bird then uses this to bite and kill the other young in the nest, those of the host.

EUROPEAN STARLING
Sturnus vulgaris

Starlings may well be building their nests by now, and if you watch the nest-hole entrance, you might find them bringing in something else along with the grass, feathers and rootlets – varying amounts of green, aromatic herbs.

Males bring them in, selecting by smell. Nobody know why. It might well be to give a good impression to a female, since the practice declines when the eggs hatch. However, recent studies suggest that the presence of aromatic herbs boosts the immune system of the youngsters.

EASTERN BLUEBIRD
Sialia sialis

This is arguably the most popular bird in North America, beloved of many thousands of people who watch pairs build their nests and raise families in specially provided bird boxes. There is even a North American Bluebird Society, formed on this day in 1978, which promotes the provision of Bluebird Trails across transects of suitable bluebird habitat: grassy areas with scattered trees, including parks.

Above: Resident most of Europe east across Eurasian to Japan, in all kinds of woodland.

Top left: Pasture in Europe east to Lake Baikal, may winter further south; introduced to North America, Australasia.

Bottom left: Open country in eastern North America and parts of Central America.

EURASIAN TREECREEPER
Certhia familiaris

Routines can be dull, but they can also be successful. Every time a treecreeper gets up in the morning, it knows exactly what it will do. It will creep up and along the trunks, branches and smaller limbs of trees, searching among crevices for its invertebrate food. It only ever creeps upwards, never head downwards, and when it reaches the top of a tree, it flies down to another nearby and forages once more with upward jumps, its vertical balance maintained by its stiffened tail. Tomorrow it will do the same, and next day, and the next. But the pathways on the trunks of trees – those irregularities in the bark, the rarely-searched fissures, the tears and holes – are infinitely variable, and the diet is plentiful. Not many birds search the limbs so thoroughly, or so close to the bark, as the mouse-like treecreeper, so it often has them to itself. There is no need for change when everything works.

EUROPEAN GREENFINCH
Chloris chloris

The greenfinch is widespread in Europe, North Africa and west Asia. This is a juvenile threatening a house sparrow.

Sometimes a bird transforms in a split second. On a cold March day, many British and European householders might see their greenfinches in bullying mode, ushering all rivals from bird feeders and then monopolizing the seed provision for themselves. Greenfinches, with their thick-set necks, frowning expression and large bills, are the heavies of the garden. There is a quick exit when they swagger into the herbaceous border.

And yet, in a carefree moment, these street fighters become street flighters. They launch into the air above the rooftops, sing a cheery trill, progress with bat-like, rushed wing-beats and often describe a circle or a figure of eight, with all the elegance of a swallow. Their transformation is complete, from brooding aggression to breezy brio, like a nightclub bouncer launching into the ballet moves of *Swan Lake*.

TUFTED TITMOUSE
Baeolophus bicolor

Residing in deciduous and mixed forests of eastern North America, these friendly, curious American birds often visit garden feeders and store food for later use.

It's March, and all around the eastern half of North America, the distinctive low, clear whistle 'Peter-Peter-Peter ...' of the tufted titmouse is starting up. A staple feature on bird feeders during the winter, the birds will now be seeking an old woodpecker hole or a bird box in which to nest.

Tufted titmice don't only sing their piercing songs but have a range of other calls, one of which is a scold, sounding like 'Chick-a-dee-dee-dee ...', made when an individual spots danger. Apparently, the birds alter the exact sound of this scold according to how dangerous the potential predator is, the rate of 'dee' notes denoting the most serious trouble. This code is sent to other tufted titmice, and the call also contains information about the sender.

GREAT CRESTED GREBE
Podiceps cristatus

A pair of great crested grebes doing the weed dance. These beautiful birds inhabit lakes and larger rivers of Eurasia and parts of Africa and Australasia.

The courtship of the great crested grebe is the ballet of lakes, ponds and rivers. Delightfully intimate and co-ordinated, it is a complex set of routines designed to form and strengthen a pair bond. The roles within the dance are entirely interchangeable, with first one bird leading and then the other, according to their respective moods.

The easiest display to see is head shaking, in which the birds face one another close up and shake their heads from side to side, often jerkily as if they were trying to shake water from their bills. This display is accompanied by a ruffling of their handsome head plumes and by grating calls. A second display is habit preening, in which a bird breaks off from head shaking to preen its back, although all it ever does is ruffle its mantle feathers lightly.

A rarer, and very exciting display is the weed dance. Here both birds submerge simultaneously and search the lake bottom for weed, a piece of which they bring to the surface held in their bill. They then swim towards each other carrying this 'gift', until they meet and rear up, breast to breast, waggling the weed for a few short moments, paddling furiously to keep upright. If it wasn't so magnificent it might be hilarious!

COMMON CHIFFCHAFF
Phylloscopus collybita

A leaf warbler of deciduous woodland in Europe and west Asia, which migrates south to winter in the northern half of Africa and the Middle East.

With the English common name chiffchaff, a Dutch name of *tjiftjaf* and a German name *Zilpzalp*, readers might notice a pattern. All these names are onomatopoeic, referring to this spritely bird's repetitive song, which in deciduous woodland is very much part of the spring chorus in many parts of Eurasia. The bird does indeed go, 'Chiff-chaff, chiff-chaff, chiff-chaff ...', repeating the disyllable 6–12 times in a row.

The scientific name is intriguing. *Phylloscopus* translates as 'examiner of leaves', which is delightfully apt for this fidgety bird of tree crowns; while *collybita* comes from the Greek *kollubistes*, which means 'money-changer.' Money-changers in Ancient Greece would have put coins of different sizes and denominations in their respective piles. The slightly different tones made by putting coins on different piles could correspond to the 'chiff' and the 'chaff' of the bird's song.

GREAT HORNED OWL
Bubo virginianus

Ubiquitous in all kinds of habitats, mainly woodland, in North America, south through Central America to northern South America.

In the depths of winter, long before any signs of spring are showing in the ground, the great horned owl begins its long breeding cycle. Its lone deep voice will be echoing across the woods and forests during the fall, and the first eggs will appear as early as January, even in temperate North America. It takes a long time to feed a clutch of owlets and prepare them for life, hence the early beginnings.

This large owl is highly adaptable and is found in all habitats right across North America. Its diet is 90 per cent mammals, from rats to hares, and it also eats large birds such as geese and ducks. These are hunted mainly in the darkness, often up until midnight and again from about 4am until daybreak. The great horned owl has exceptional night vision for this purpose.

It occasionally catches extra food, which it stores away. On a cold day like today, when retrieving the cache, it might have to sit on the carcass for ten minutes or so, allowing its body heat to thaw the meal!

27ᵀᴴ MARCH

WILLOW WARBLER
Phylloscopus trochilus

This week sees the first arrivals of willow warblers into the breeding grounds of northern Europe and Asia. For many birdwatchers and country folk, their sweet song is the quintessence of authentic spring, the truest refrain of the changing season. The song is a gentle descending scale, sung as if a little distracted, blown away somewhat by the spring breeze. It has been described charmingly as being like the breeze taking the shawl off a lady's shoulder.

28ᵀᴴ MARCH

BURROWING OWL
Athene cunicularia

A familiar bird in the southern and western United States, Central and South America, the burrowing owl lives up to its name, living in – guess where! – burrows in the ground. They mainly eat insects, and one of their favourite prey items is large dung beetles. And, while the owls will go foraging for these, they also have a trick to make life easier. The birds go and collect mammal dung and drop it around the entrance to their burrows, hoping to attract prey to them, rather than the other way around!

GREAT BUSTARD
Otis tarda

Above: Plains and semi-desert in Europe and west Asia, where resident; Central and east Asian birds winter further south.

Top left: Willow warblers are found throughout northern Eurasia; winters in sub-Saharan Africa.

Bottom left: An owl of the grasslands and prairies throughout much of the Americas.

On the open plains and steppes where the huge great bustard lives, it is possible to misidentify it from a distance – but only for a sheep. And in those circumstances, if it takes off, you might find yourself doing a double-take. In truth, though, taking to the air is an effort, for the great bustard is generally regarded as the heaviest of all birds to fly. It weighs up to 21kg (over 46lb), although the usual range is rather less: 6–19kg (13–42lb). Various other species rival the great bustard for mass, including other large bustards, swans and condors.

Once airborne, the great bustard looks magnificent in flight, with its slow, imperious wing-beats and its neck held straight out in front. To improve the spectacle further, birds often fly together in flocks, and sometimes it is possible see the extraordinary size difference between adult males and females – the latter being three times lighter.

In spring, the great bustard performs a magnificent 'foam bath' display, in which it seems to turn its plumage inside out. It looks as if someone is shaking a white carpet free of dust.

DUNNOCK
Prunella modularis

'It's always the quiet ones' is an expression that could have been coined with the dunnock in mind. Resident in scrub, gardens and mountains of western Europe, the bird migrates to eastern Europe, wintering to the south.

The quintessential small brown bird, the dunnock is common in Western Europe. Modest in its habits, it never bickers at the feeder or jumps the queue. It sings its simple warble almost apologetically.

Its modesty was noted by an Irish clergyman, the Reverend Frederick Morris, who wrote admiringly in his book, *A History of British Birds* (1850–57): 'Unobtrusive, quiet and retiring, without being shy, humble and homely in its deportment and habits, sober and unpretending in its dress, while still neat and graceful, the dunnock exhibits a pattern which many of a higher grade might imitate, with advantage to themselves ...'

Had a higher grade taken the reverend literally, chaos would have ensued in the parish. DNA and ringing studies from the 1980s onwards showed that the dunnock has the most extraordinary sex life, involving multiple partners, multiple matings, infidelity galore and deception. It turns out that the dunnock was faking its modesty.

BARN SWALLOW
Hirundo rustica

The national bird of Austria and Estonia roosts in large communities – sometimes over a million strong. It favours all kinds of habitats throughout a vast breeding range across North America and Eurasia, and winters in Africa, India and South America.

In the 4th century BCE, Aristotle wrote, 'One swallow makes not a spring', but there is little doubt that the saying was being used long before that. Oddly, the version most used these days in English is, 'One swallow doesn't make a summer', which paints a much bleaker picture.

In fact the phrase is used all over the world because this songbird has a uniquely wide distribution, breeding in Eurasia and North America, and wintering in the summers of South America and Africa. It is the quintessential worldwide migrant. It also has one of the longest migrations among smaller birds.

In the past, when the idea that birds might undertake transcontinental migrations was never even entertained, people seriously postulated that swallows might overwinter by hibernating at the bottom of ponds, as some frogs do. The reality is, of course, even more remarkable.

SNOWY SHEATHBILL
Chionis albus

I f you are reading about today's bird during breakfast or some other meal, here is a warning. What follows is disgusting.

Sheathbills hail from the Antarctic, but have none of the charm of penguins. Sheathbills do like penguins, though – at least, they enjoy eating their dead chicks or some feathers. They also relish being in the company of seals, and enjoy eating afterbirths, nasal mucus (which they snatch, literally, from under the seals' noses) and the blood from gaping wounds. Lovely.

2ᴺᴰ APRIL

RUFF
Calidris pugnax

T he ruff is a Eurasian shorebird with a complex breeding behaviour, which involves males spending much of the day on communal display grounds, called leks. Females visit leks to mate briefly and they then disappear duly inseminated and incubate the eggs and raise the young alone.

Since male ruffs only have to contribute sperm, they are well endowed. Their testes in spring account for 5 per cent of their body weight – more than their brain.

COMMON CRANE
Grus grus

Above: In bogs and wetlands across Eurasia; highly migratory, wintering in Spain, Africa, India and south-east Asia.

Top left: Coasts of Antarctic and South Georgia.

Bottom left: Breeds on tundra and meadows across northern Eurasia; winters Africa, south-east Asia, Oceania.

Many birds sing in the spring, but few trumpet the season's arrival in the majestic manner of the common crane. A tall bird with a long neck, the crane has a specially extended windpipe which coils within the breastbone, amplifying its already loud, clanging call. It can be heard many kilometres away, especially on a cold, still, frosty morning.

The unmistakable V-shaped formations of cranes in flight have long been admired, and the birds' regular migrations make them harbingers of the seasons. During the first week of April, much of the Scandinavian population stops on its way north at Lake Hornborga in southern Sweden, almost 20,000 birds in all. The comings and goings of the huge birds, the promise of spring, the orchestra of wild bugles and the formations in the sky, all combine to create an awe-inspiring bird spectacle.

SONG THRUSH
Turdus philomelos

Oh, to be in England
Now that April's there,
And whoever wakes in England
Sees, some morning, unaware,
That the lowest boughs and the brushwood sheaf
Round the elm-tree bole are in tiny leaf,
While the chaffinch sings on the orchard bough
In England – now!

And after April, when May follows,
And the whitethroat builds, and all the swallows!
Hark, where my blossomed pear-tree in the hedge
Leans to the field and scatters on the clover
Blossoms and dewdrops – at the bent spray's edge –
That's the wise thrush; he sings each song twice over,
Lest you should think he never could recapture
The first fine careless rapture!
And though the fields look rough with hoary dew,
All will be gay when noontide wakes anew
The buttercups, the little children's dower
– Far brighter than this gaudy melon-flower!

This songbird lives in woodland and gardens in western Europe; further east to Central Asia, where it is migratory

This poem, 'Home Thoughts from Abroad', was written by the English romantic poet Robert Browning in 1845. One of the most popular poems in the UK, it describes a feeling of homesickness and pining to be elsewhere. The poet was staying in northern Italy when he wrote it.

Browning was obviously alert to birds – his description of the song thrush's repetitive song is peerless (although you could argue that the song is sung 'thrice over'). But had he listened more carefully to the birds around him in Italy, he would have had no problem at all observing chaffinch, whitethroat, swallow and song thrush, all of which are common there!

COMMON WHITETHROAT
Sylvia communis

Perky and full of zest, the common whitethroat abounds in spring in the hedgerows and scrub of Eurasia. It sings a very short, scratchy phrase from a perch, ruffling its gleaming white throat feathers, and at times it appears as if the male has covered his chin in shaving foam. It also has a song-flight, similarly scratchy but longer, while the bird seems to swing from an invisible elastic string.

6TH APRIL

SOUTHERN CASSOWARY
Casuarius casuarius

You should be wary of the cassowary. On this day in 1926 an Australian teenager was slashed on the throat and killed by the claw of a cassowary and in New Guinea, where the birds are frequently hunted, an unknown number of people have lost their lives. A few zoo keepers have also had fatal encounters. The cassowary is armed with a 4in (10cm) razor-sharp claw on the middle of its three toes, and if it kicks accurately with either foot, these weapons can inflict terrible injuries.

Top left: The size of a great tit, this warbler spends his summers in Europe and west Asia; winters in sub-Saharan Africa.

Bottom left: This solitary ground-nesting bird is resident of dense rainforests of northern Australia, New Guinea and the Aru Islands.

Right: This piscivore is highly adapted to catch his prey and can be found in lakes, wetlands and coast, almost worldwide.

OSPREY
Pandion haliaetus

Found throughout the world, the osprey is a hawk that has specialized in catching fish by plunge-diving into the water from above. The bird soars at moderate height over fresh or salt water and, when it spots potential prey, it either hovers first to find its bearings, or just plunges straight in, talons first, with its wings held at its sides.

The osprey's feet have evolved a network of spikes on their undersides and these, together with long, curved claws, help the raptor to hold on to prey, which is slippery and, not surprisingly, somewhat reluctant to be hauled away and eaten. The raptor flies off with the fish held, torpedo-style, under its body.

SEDGE WARBLER
Acrocephalus schoenobaenus

Summer visitor to wetland edges from western Europe to central Asia; winters in sub-Saharan Africa.

This small brown bird with the perky song arrives in Europe in April, after a winter spent in tropical Africa. Over the years it has proven to be a fruitful species to study. For example, studies on sedge warblers were among the first to prove that females can be prone preferentially to select males with larger song repertoires than more limited ones; captive females performed more soliciting postures when listening to rich variety! Another classic study showed that the number of song-flights performed by a male was in inverse proportion to the number of parasites in its plumage. Males are also unusual for halting song production as soon as they are paired, proving the song has more of a role in attracting a mate than in marking its territory. It's all revelatory stuff!

WESTERN YELLOW WAGTAIL
Motacilla flava

Summer visitor to open habitats and wetland across the eastern half of Eurasia; winters in sub-Saharan Africa.

When is a yellow wagtail not a yellow wagtail? The answer is when it is blue-headed or black-headed, grey-headed or Spanish, or ashy-headed or Sykes', or several other variations. The yellow wagtail is one of the most racially variable of European birds, the main, but not only difference being in the head colour of the males. Most races mix on migration and, to some extent in their winter quarters. Many hybridize freely, so they cannot be considered different species.

A summer visitor to Europe and Asia, this long-legged beauty, which often sports stunning buttery-yellow plumage, is common in many types of wetland habitat. It often feeds at the feet of cattle and horses, catching flies and other insects stirred up by their hooves, and this can be a good way to find it. It translates this ability to its wintering grounds in tropical Africa, where it will sometimes feed at the feet of more exotic animals.

EASTERN TOWHEE
Pipilo erythrophthalmus

An untold number of novice American birders are grateful to the simple sounds of the eastern towhee for their introduction to the tricky art of learning birdsong. The unmistakable song-phrase, 'Drink your teeeeee ...' is one of the very easiest to learn; the most common call, 'Tow-ee', is just a repetition of the name. In addition, this is a handsome and distinctive bird, a beginner's delight.

JAPANESE BUSH WARBLER
Horornis diphone

Every culture has its iconic songbirds, and in the case of Japan nothing can rival the melodic Japanese bush warbler. This is a very noisy bird, and its song has a loud, rising tone that explodes into three fast, liquid notes. Called *uguisu* in Japanese, it is associated with the coming of spring, and is represented in many traditional Japanese poems. A euphonious female announcer, for example at sports events or political rallies, is known as a *uguisu-jō*.

EURASIAN SKYLARK
Alauda arvensis

Above: A bird of open fields and grassland over much of Eurasia; northern and eastern populations migrate south; introduced to Australia and New Zealand.

Top left: A male and female towhee – the latter being brown where the males are black. They reside in brush and shrubland in eastern North America; northern populations are migratory.

Bottom left: A warbler of scrubby habitats in Japan.

Much loved by people throughout Europe, the skylark is celebrated for its remarkable song, and ecstatic outpouring of shrill notes, a veritable spate of syllables that are so excitable that they almost trip out. The lark's flight, rising high to 30m (100ft), undulating on the spot and then gradually falling, has been immortalized in verse and music. Percy Bysshe Shelley, in 1820 wrote in 'To a Skylark':

Hail to thee, blithe Spirit!
Bird thou never wert,
That from Heaven, or near it,
Pourest thy full heart
In profuse strains of unpremeditated art.

Higher still and higher
From the earth thou springest
Like a cloud of fire;
The blue deep thou wingest,
And singing still dost soar, and soaring ever singest ...

The lark's song was also celebrated in Ralph Vaughan Williams's *The Lark Ascending* (1914), one of the most popular pieces of classical music in the UK.

EURASIAN BLACKCAP
Sylvia atricapilla

The blackcap lays 4–6 eggs in a low nest, often in the brambles. It prefers the deciduous woodlands of Europe and west Asia; northern populations migrate west or south, some to sub-Saharan Africa.

What's a female blackcap to do? The airwaves of spring are full of melodies, sweet and jabbering. Everywhere there are male blackcaps inciting suitors to approach them and pair up. Pairing, as is usual in the bird world, is a matter of female choice.

Males singing at a high rate of between 160 and 180 song-phrases per hour, possess the best and safest territories, with rich and dense vegetation where the nest can be secreted away. Males singing at a lower rate, those managing 80–100 song-phrases per hour, don't have such plush territories, instead they have a more open aspect. However, these males do make a greater contribution towards helping feed the chicks in the nest.

ELF OWL
Micrathene whitneyi

Have you ever wondered what the smallest owl in the world is? It's the elf owl of the southern USA and Mexico, just 12–14cm (around 5in) long and weighing 35–55g (1–2oz). Not surprisingly, it tends only to eat invertebrates such as moths, beetles and crickets.

The elf owl usually nests in the hole made by a woodpecker in a tree or, more famously, in a giant saguaro cactus. With the owls being small, they risk being caught by predators themselves. That's why they are thought to associate regularly with species of tree ants. The ants live in the same place and, when an intruder approaches the hole, they attack and bite the unwanted guest. However, the ants leave the owls entirely alone.

The saguaro cactus, growing to around 12m (40ft) makes a good nest site for this miniature owl, who resides in the deserts or thorn and scrubby forests of south-west North America and Mexico.

BLACK GROUSE
Lyrurus tetrix

Frequenting northern and parts of western Europe and much of western, central and eastern Asia, this grouse is not ashamed to display himself for the ladies.

There exists a certain type of entertainment where, mainly to the benefit of watching ladies, troupes of attractive men parade in front of their audience and display some of their wares. Something similar takes place on the moorland and forest edges of Eurasia when, early each morning in the breeding season and again in the autumn, troupes of male black grouse, usually 10–20 of them, gather for much the same reason.

A group of displaying male birds is called a lek. On the display ground, or arena, each bird has its own small territory. Males spend much time fighting over the best site for these territories, which is often a small eminence or platform. When a female visits, she finds that the males have self-selected. The owner of the best territory is the top bird. Ignoring all others, every female attracted to the lek makes a beeline for him.

Apart from copulation, the male plays no role in reproduction. Good genes are enough. The female departs inseminated with quality DNA.

BLACK WHEATEAR
Oenanthe leucura

This nest may look like a mess to us, but those stones were placed deliberately. This bird lives in the dry rocky areas and scrub of Iberia and North Africa.

Are female black wheatears the choosiest birds in the world? Not only do they listen to a male singing and watch his flight display when choosing a potential mate, they also rate him on the basis of how he behaves during nest-building.

The black wheatear builds its nest in a rock crevice or cave. To start with the male doesn't add to the structure, but instead he brings in decorations, in the form of hard objects such as stones. These have no obvious purpose, except to demonstrate how good he is at carrying things and, presumably, to provide some measure of his physiological health.

Remarkably, the male's stone-collecting efforts – he may bring in 400 or so – help the female decide how many eggs to lay and how often to copulate. If the effort is good, the clutch will be greater than if the male brings only a few or none at all.

Yellow Warbler
Setophaga petechia

Summer visitor to wet thickets and scrub in North America; winters in Central and northern South America.

The dawn chorus is in full swing, and few North American birds sing at such intensity as the effervescent yellow warbler, which may get going an hour before sunrise. This beauty has a particularly intriguing pattern of delivery. Each individual male has about 10–17 slightly different song types, and during the dawn bout he will sing most of them, mixed together. These songs will be interspersed with the bird's most familiar call, known as a 'chip' note. After about 30 minutes, however, the singer will calm down somewhat and switch to just one song-type, repeated for the rest of the day.

Remarkably, there is a record of a bird which had one song type that was only used once in 5,628 songs. It obviously wasn't his favourite.

HOUSE WREN
Troglodytes aedon

Summer visitor to brush, hedgerow and gardens in North America; winters in the Gulf States south to Mexico.

Can there be a more delightful description of any bird's song than that of Neltje Blanchan, writing in 1903 about North America's ubiquitous house wren?

'like some little mountain spring that, having been imprisoned by winter ice, now bubbles up in the spring sunshine, and goes rippling along over the pebbles, tumbling over itself in merry cascades, so this little wren's song bubbles, ripples, cascades in a miniature torrent of ecstasy.'

Indeed, this is a bird much more often heard than seen. Much more often – it is frequently heard as the 'wildtrack' background to many hundreds of TV broadcasts, from dramas to commercials, and not always in the United States, either!

RED-WINGED BLACKBIRD
Agelaius phoeniceus

Above: Breeds in any wet marshy or brush habitat in North America; migratory in north of range, Great Lakes northwards.

Top right: Sunbitterns fish the streams and rivers in Central and northern South America.

Bottom right: Coots live in the wetlands of Eurasia, Australia, New Zealand, Indian subcontinent.

It's an age-old problem. Does a female choose sexy or reliable?

The red-winged blackbird is an abundant North American bird of marshes, fields and built-up areas. Males set up territories in the spring, and in a restricted space such as a swamp, there are only so many territories that can be divided up among a surfeit of hopefuls. Inevitably, the highest-quality males obtain the best real estate, those parts of the marsh with the densest vegetation or the richest feeding places. Some obtain inferior territories; others get nothing at all.

In studies, females have tended to go for the males with the best territories. There is no surprise there, except for one thing. Invariably, these females would be choosing to share his charms – and his DNA – with other females. Even though subordinate males were available for an exclusive relationship in which they would put their undivided heart and soul into helping feed the chicks, these males were often neglected. It seems that the females preferred a sexy male who would not be much use in feeding the chicks, to a less attractive male who would make a hard-working father.

SUNBITTERN
Eurypyga helias

The sunbittern is a peculiar bird found along rivers in tropical America. It is shy and easily overlooked, until it feels threatened. It then performs a spectacular frontal display, in which the wings are spread to reveal their extraordinary pattern, including the large chestnut 'eyes'. The tail is also spread to meet the wings, making the bird look far larger than it is.

COMMON COOT
Fulica atra

Common coots swim in the water and look rather like ducks, but their bills are different as they are not flattened. Coots also lack webbing between the toes. Coots have an interesting, and utterly ruthless, way of coping if there isn't enough food for their chicks. They typically lay 5–7 eggs, and from these hatch black balls of fluff with ugly red head-dresses and a bad attitude, which beg constantly all day long. If the brood is too large for the available food, the adults attack the weakest chicks instead of feeding them. The ones that don't die from their wounds cease begging and die of starvation.

GREAT SPOTTED CUCKOO
Clamator glandarius

This cuckoo spends its summers in heath and open scrub in south-west and south-east Europe; widespread Africa.

This is Europe's 'other' cuckoo, less famous than the common cuckoo and mainly confined to the Mediterranean region. It lays its eggs in the nests of other birds, in the same way as the common cuckoo, but there are many intriguing differences in the way it goes about it.

For a start, the host species are completely different. The common cuckoo famously selects small, insectivorous foster parents for its young, but the great spotted cuckoo's favoured hosts are magpies and carrion crows. These much more formidable foes mean that, instead of a silent, secret visit by a lone female, the great spotted cuckoo's strategy is to approach the host nest as a pair, noisily. The male distracts the parents, while the female steals in to lay the egg.

The female great spotted cuckoo doesn't remove a host egg, but instead may attempt to chip a host egg with her bill and lay her own hard-shelled eggs on the host eggs, intending to crack them. In another key difference, the young cuckoo doesn't evict its nest-mates, but instead attempts to out-compete them, hatching much earlier and being noisier. The result is that the crow's own nestlings often starve.

This shows that there are always several ways to be a parasite.

WHITE-CROWNED SPARROW
Zonotrichia leucophrys

This pretty sparrow breeds in tundra and meadows in northern and montane North America; winters in fields from the Great Lakes to Mexico.

Many people think that birds only have one song, and that a particular sort of bird in one place will have the same song as everywhere else. However, this isn't the case. Songs vary regionally, and a good many species have dialects.

The white-crowned sparrow is one such bird, and in its case the dialects are very distinctive. So clear are the borders that birds singing one dialect may live just across the road from singers of a neighbouring dialect; individuals that straddle the border are sometimes bilingual.

Dialects are particularly obvious in white-crowned sparrows because each individual male only has one song type. This it learns from its father and his neighbours, maintaining the dialect down through the generations. So, a white-crowned sparrow from Los Angeles will be recognizable as such, and distinct from one from San Francisco. And even the birds in different neighbourhoods in the same locality will be obvious.

EASTERN KINGBIRD

Tyrannus tyrannus

Summers in many open habitats in North America away from the arid south-west; winters in western South America. This bird is mobbing an osprey!

They say that everybody needs good neighbours, but the eastern kingbird has no intention of being anything of the sort. This widespread summer visitor to North America makes life difficult for many of its local residents, earning it the well-deserved scientific name *Tyrannus*, the tyrant.

The problem is that it doesn't like its nest being threatened, even if the threat is only perceived. It will fly at hawks of all kinds, harassing them away from its territory. It will go for blue jays, crows, squirrels and often, people, swooping down furiously and raising its red crown feathers. It can be surprisingly intimidating – and that, of course, is the idea.

MEADOW PIPIT
Anthus pratensis

A ground-nesting bird in the grassland and tundra of Europe and west Asia that winters in the warmer climes of North Africa and the Middle East.

Meadow pipits are throwaway birds in a consumer society: the feathered plastic, the small change. Nobody takes much notice of them. They are quintessentially small, brown, streaky and dull. They walk instead of hopping, which is tolerably interesting, but largely ignored. On the northern grasslands and moorlands where they abound, meadow pipits are more takeaways than throwaways, snacks for a range of local predators.

In spring, though, pipits transform into flight-dancers. They lift from the ground on shimmering wings, singing their song of repeated notes, which can sound like one of those especially persistent alarm clocks. They rise up in the air, suddenly cease the beating of their wings, and then raise their tail and hold their wings steady as they glide slowly down back to the ground. As they fall, so does the pitch of their notes.

It is a performance that demonstrates even loose change can add up to a lot.

YELLOW-RUMPED WARBLER
Setophaga coronata

Several warblers from a plate by Audubon: (1 and 2) 'Audubon's' yellow-rumped, (3 and 4) hermit and (5 and 6) black-throated gray. Breeds in coniferous forests in the north; winters widely.

The yellow-rumped warbler leads a double life. As a breeding bird it stretches far into the Arctic, populating remote areas of the taiga zone that are dominated by vast forests of coniferous trees. Here, very few people come across it. In the winter, however, streams of these warblers spill down into the heart of North America, where they can be found almost everywhere, including parks and gardens. They change their diet to include berries, and they thrive from New England to the coast of British Columbia.

This bird also leads a double life in its appearance. The populations of the west, Audubon's warblers, have markedly different breeding finery from those of the east, myrtle warblers, so much so that they used to be treated as separate species. In the autumn, however, they all moult into a similar pattern, a classic in the 'confusing fall warbler' category.

GOLDEN-WINGED WARBLER
Vermivora chrysoptera

In 2014, a group of male golden-winged warblers fitted with geolocators appeared at their breeding grounds in eastern Tennessee, as their predecessors would have done thousands of times before, arriving between 13 and 27 April. This spring, however, was different. A powerful storm was heading their way, one that was destructive enough to kill 35 people.

What did the birds do? Incredibly, a day or so before the storm struck, they evacuated the area in which they had just arrived, and took refuge 400 miles (644km) to the south, in Texas. They stayed there for a few days, then simply flew back to their breeding grounds and started singing again as if nothing had happened.

The big question is: how did they know the storm was coming? Nobody can know for sure, but it is as if the birds could hear the approaching weather disturbance emitting low-pitched rumbles or infrasounds.

NORTHERN JACANA
Jacana spinosa

Does life feel rocky at times? If so, spare a thought for the northern jacana. This bird spends most of its life scuttling over lily pads. It has remarkably elongated toes to spread its weight, to ensure it does not fall into the water. Even the nest of a jacana is built on floating vegetation.

The gender roles of jacanas are reversed. Males perform most breeding duties, including incubating the eggs and looking after the young.

ROSS'S GULL
Rhodostethia rosea

With its ethereal, rose-washed plumage and High Arctic habitat, Ross's gull has cast a spell over admirers ever since the bird's discovery in 1823. On an expedition to the Russian Arctic in 1879, a group of adventurers found their vessel trapped in pack ice. The survivors had to abandon ship and embark on the perilous trek 320km (200 miles) south in the hope of reaching safety. Throughout this life-or-death journey, the expedition naturalist, Raymond Newcomb, protected three Ross's gull skins under his shirt.

BROWN-HEADED COWBIRD
Molothrus ater

Residing in the plains, arable areas and suburbs of North America, northern populations migrate south, as far as Mexico. Here, a brown-headed cowbird has laid one of her speckled eggs among the eggs of an eastern phoebe.

Surely one of the most remarkable birds in North America, and perhaps the world, the brown-headed cowbird is also one of the most unpopular. The reason? It is a brood parasite. It lays its eggs in the nests of many other bird species, and at times makes the common cuckoo (see page 127) look like an amateur.

A single female brown-headed cowbird may lay more than 70 eggs in a season. If they all hatch and grow up, they will each out-compete the young of their host species, which may starve, causing huge losses. While many cuckoo females are host-specific, a single cowbird female will use many hosts. Overall, brown-headed cowbirds have been recorded laying eggs in the nests of 220 species, and of these, 114 have been successful hosts, raising a cowbird to fledging.

The most 'popular' species are yellow warbler, song sparrow, red-eyed vireo, chipping sparrow and eastern phoebe. Some birds, such as the American robin and grey catbird, always reject them. Success may depend on when a cowbird lays; if the clutch is already complete, it might be too late.

The damage done by cowbirds is continent-wide, but the local effects can be especially damaging. In Michigan, for example, cowbirds frequently lay in the nests of the ultra-rare Kirtland's warbler (see page 155), endangering the future of a species that is already endangered.

MARBLED MURRELET
Brachyramphus marmoratus

Breeds in old-growth forests of the Pacific Coast of North America; winters at sea.

One of the enduring mysteries of North American ornithology for more than 100 years was 'Where do marbled murrelets nest?' This small sea bird related to puffins and murres (guillemots), spends most of its time offshore diving for small fish and crustaceans.

Due to the fact that this is a sea bird, from a family of sea birds, it came as a big surprise that the marbled murrelet actually nests in the tops of trees in coastal forests, some up to 6km (4 miles) inland. Birds were found as high as 12m (40ft) off the ground on thick, horizontal branches. The parents often visit the nest in the darkness before sunrise.

As these nesting sites were not discovered until 1974, this was one of the last North American birds to have its nest described.

EURASIAN CUCKOO
Cuculus canorus

The common cuckoo works its deeds across Europe and Asia; winters in sub-Saharan Africa and southern Asia, in forests.

Nobody knows if there ever was a 'Scene by the Brook' in real life that inspired the great composer Beethoven to immortalize the country birds of Vienna in the second movement of his peerless 6th symphony, the ever-tuneful 'Pastoral'. But if ever the cuckoo, nightingale and quail sung together, it would be in the first week of May, at dawn or dusk.

The simplest of songs, the two-note 'Cucko-oo', hides a highly complex lifestyle. The volume belies the cuckoo's secret mission to parasitize smaller birds, bluster concealing espionage. The males couldn't be more obvious, singing so sonorously that they create an atmosphere just by opening their mouths. The females, on the other hand, keep silent watch from cryptic perches, monitoring the breeding progress of potential foster parents. The parents leave the nest, the hour comes, the cuckoo strikes. The cuckoo clocks another hit. The cycle continues.

LESSER SPOTTED EAGLE
Clanga pomarina

Taking the 'heir and a spare' concept to its limit, the lesser spotted eagle breeds on the steppes of western Asia and eastern Europe, wintering in Africa.

How's this for a breeding strategy? You lay two eggs, two little bundles of your DNA, your genetic future, your investment. You then incubate them, warm under your skin, apparently cherished.

However, you have essentially condemned one of them to death already. Rather than beginning incubation when both eggs have been laid, you instead begin incubating as soon as the first egg comes. When the second egg is laid, three days after the first, it is far behind its sibling in development. It hatches three days later, by which time the first born is bigger, heavier and stronger. So begins an uneven struggle for attention and food, and there's only one winner. The first born takes all the food and will eventually starve its sibling to death. It may even eat it.

Every successful family of lesser spotted eagles raises a single chick, and virtually all the second born chicks die. It's known as the Cain and Abel conflict, and takes a huge toll on eaglets every year.

COMMON SWIFT
Apus apus

Sweeps across the summer skies of Eurasia; winters in Africa.

Swifts are among the most aerial of birds. So small are their feet, on which all four toes face forwards, they are unable to perch or stand – indeed, the scientific name *Apus* means 'without feet'. These birds never land on anything solid except to visit the nest, which is built in a hole in on a cliff or tall building, or by accident. Since the birds don't breed until they are 3–4 years old, youngsters will migrate all the way from Africa to Europe, plying the summer skies for zephyr-borne insects and touring the colonies, but never setting foot on solid ground until they are back in Africa again.

As they are adapted to catching flying insects, which they snatch with the bill in flight having spotted them first, swifts are always at the mercy of the weather. Recent studies have shown that the birds can tell, by a drop in insect density, when a cold front is coming. Rather than cope with adverse conditions, they will instead evacuate the area and fly in a great loop to avoid it, a journey that may take them 2,000km (1,200 miles).

NORTHERN MOCKINGBIRD
Mimus polyglottos

At home in the suburbs and fields of North America, commonest in southern part of the USA south to Mexico.

The much-loved mockingbird is the chosen emblem of several US states – Texas, Arkansas, Tennessee, Mississippi and Florida. It is ingrained in the affections of those in the Deep South, although these days it has also expanded its range northwards into New England. It is abundant and easy to see, with its bold grey, black and white pattern, fearless demeanour and long, mobile tail.

Its greatest asset, however, is its remarkable song, which includes not only much of its own creation, but also multiple copies of the songs of other birds. A famous individual in a Boston park was apparently able to copy 39 other bird songs and 50 calls. The song is given with great gusto and virtuosity and confers an unmistakable *joie de vivre* upon the atmosphere.

The song has been cherished for many centuries. A delightful native American myth speaks of the mockingbird distributing different languages to different peoples back in the mists of time.

Parts of North
America, in
marshes; some
migrate south to
Mexico in winter.

MARSH WREN
Cistothorus palustris

You wouldn't choose to be a marsh wren. They have one of the most frantic breeding seasons of any bird. Their problem appears to be that fact that they live in marshes. Marshes are always limited in extent, and this means that everything a marsh wren needs is in limited supply. To get anywhere the male, especially, needs to be ultra-competitive.

These North American songsters are constantly under pressure to sing, and during April and May they will sometimes perform incessantly, day and night. A male marsh wren may have to learn up to 200 song types to get ahead. He will also feverishly build nests for the female to choose, sometimes up to 22 of them. He also needs to select the richest part of the marsh if he is to attract a mate. Nearly half of all males will attract more than one female, which leaves many without a mate at all.

Bizarrely, amidst all the kerfuffle, both sexes routinely destroy the eggs and nests of other marsh wrens, and even of other species, presumably to reduce competition. They will pierce eggs with their bills and pull nests apart.

How any marsh wren manages to cope and breed successfully in such a frenzied atmosphere is a good question.

COMMON NIGHTINGALE
Luscinia megarhynchos

The nightingale is one of the world's most celebrated small brown birds. It has an exceptional song, full-throated, rich and with a staggering dynamic range, from a shout to a whisper. The bird's capacity to sing at night (although it sings by day, too), and its concentrated song at the sweetest time of year, when the days are still lengthening, temperatures are increasing and the flowers of spring are at their most opulent, makes hearing a nightingale more an event than an ornithological endeavour. Wherever it occurs, the nightingale is adored, and has inspired much romantic literature, from Western Europe to Persia.

One of literature's most famous poems is John Keats' 'Ode to a Nightingale', written by the Englishman on the edge of Hampstead Heath, London, in 1819.

My heart aches, and a drowsy numbness pains
My sense, as though of hemlock I had drunk,
Or emptied some dull opiate to the drains
One minute past, and Lethe-wards had sunk:
'Tis not through envy of thy happy lot,
But being too happy in thine happiness,
That thou, light-winged Dryad of the trees,
In some melodious plot
Of beechen green, and shadows numberless,
Singest of summer in full-throated ease.

It has a melancholic theme, comparing the nightingale's everlasting song, heard down the generations, to man's – and Keats' – mortality. Sadly, fortunes of the local nightingales did not echo those of the poem. They have long gone from the Hampstead area, now swallowed up by urbanization, never to return.

COPPERSMITH BARBET
Psilopogon haemacephalus

Coppersmith barbets create large nest cavities in the woods and forests of Indian subcontinent east to south-east Asia and Sundas. The young often live at home and make sure they roost early to prevent their parents from refusing entry.

In the forest or woodland of India or south-east Asia, at any time of year, you might hear a loud 'tok..tok..tok' emanating from somewhere above you. The sound recalls the banging from a building site or, more specifically, the sound of a coppersmith striking metal. Uttered at various speeds, and seemingly nonstop, this is the advertising call of the coppersmith barbet, one of the staple background sounds of this part of the world.

Barbets are a family of fruit-eating tropical birds famous for their noisy calls, and they also have another curious characteristic – sabotage. They excavate a hole in a tree for their nest, which is hard work, taking two weeks or so. When one species of barbet comes across a hole in progress or being used it often simply comes in and wrecks it. In the case of the coppersmith barbet, its nemesis in India is the white-cheeked barbet (*Psilopogon viridis*). The larger bird will evict the 'rightful' pair and enlarge the cavity, or simply spoil the structure.

FLORIDA SCRUB-JAY
Aphelocoma coerulescens

Found only in
oak scrub on
well-drained
soils in Central
Florida.

Found in just one state of the USA, and nowhere else in the world, the
Florida scrub-jay is also thoroughly fussy about its habitat. It needs oak
scrub, on a sandy soil, surrounded by pine forests. Oak scrub is a rare and
fragmented community only found in a few places.

Young Florida scrub-jays, therefore, are hemmed in by their own species'
restrictive lifestyle. They cannot just leave their home scrub and make a
living in another state or another country. Instead they must stay at home.
Few individuals ever move more than a few kilometres in their entire lives.

The home scrub is also forever full of other scrub-jay families, with no
empty space for a bird to move in. So instead, young scrub-jays remain
with their parents and devote themselves to the family cause. When the
parents reproduce again, they help with feeding their younger brothers
and sisters. They might do this next year, too, and the year after. Theirs
is a world of limited horizons.

NORTHERN CARDINAL
Cardinalis cardinalis

May is the height of the breeding season for one of North America's most popular birds, the cardinal. Throughout much of eastern North America, its glorious song dominates the soundscape of back yards, parks and woodlands. During this time, the song can have special meaning. Scientists have found that female cardinals sing to males from the nest. If a male approaches the nest singing, the female will match his song type if she wishes him to come with food, or keep silent if she prefers him to stay away.

11TH MAY

GREATER RHEA
Rhea americana

The rhea is the South American version of the ostrich, living in similar open grassy habitats, although the two birds are very different in anatomy, the rhea having a feathered neck, three toes instead of two and quite different types of feathers – they are soft and are often used as dusters in local homes.

In the breeding season, males take on all duties of nest-building, incubation and rearing the young.

COMMON SNIPE
Gallinago gallinago

Snipe are crypto-ninjas. Their plumage is a classic example of cryptic colouration and pattern, hide-and-seek in feathered art. They move slowly and gently, keeping under cover where they can. They don't call often, but if flushed by danger they make a sound like an irritable kiss, if such a thing is possible.

Yet, in the mild darkness of a spring night, the snipe is unleashed. It abandons its undercover day job and launches itself into the air. It zooms in circles, in figures of eight, up and down, set free. As the wind rushes past, the snipe spreads its outermost tail feathers and produces a buzzing sound which, as it happens, sounds unerringly like the baa of a sheep – and since the snipe is often found in damp corners of sheep country, many a human returning from the pub after closing time is convinced he has heard an aerial herbivore.

But no, it's a snipe, whizzing in the wind.

SPOTTED FLYCATCHER
Muscicapa striata

This flycatcher takes his name – *striata* – from his streaked crown. He spends the summers in open woodland in Europe and west Asia; winters in sub-Saharan Africa.

Never mind air-traffic control, in summer the airspace of Europe is buzzing with myriad flying insects of innumerable species, going about their daily business at every speed, in every direction, at every height up to the treetops and beyond, on errands ranging from the simple to the technical. Into this airy smorgasbord comes the spotted flycatcher, the latest of our common summer migrants to arrive, not present in any great number until May. It is happiest when the holiday traffic is heaviest, unlike the rest of us.

The spotted flycatcher's signature technique is to set off from an elevated perch, snap an insect in flight, then return to the same, or another nearby watchpoint. It's very simple and works well from the shores of the Mediterranean to the Arctic Circle.

GREAT GREY SHRIKE
Lanius excubitor

Living in open habitats in parts of Europe, Africa, the Middle East and Asia east to China. This one has impaled a vole – a large meal.

Along their evolutionary journey, songbirds were bound to turn rogue at some point. The result is a family called the shrikes, whose bills have developed into hook-tipped weapons and whose perching feet have claws that are sharp, curved and deadly. They have also evolved the unusual and gruesome habit of hanging up their kills on natural hooks, such as thorns, spines and twigs, as well as man-made hooks like barbed wire. When hunting is good, a shrike's lair may contain a mortuary of hanging bodies, cached for use later, earning shrikes the nickname of 'butcher birds'. These caches may include the bodies of large insects, small mammals or even other birds.

Male shrikes work hard in the breeding season to catch food for their mate and family, and their caches are distributed in patches over the territory. Sometimes a hunter may procure something extra-special, such as a heavy-bodied vole or similar. In these cases, the male might not bring it to his mate – indeed, he might hide it away. This will be intended for a different purpose – to solicit a sexual liaison with a different female!

EURASIAN GOLDEN ORIOLE *Oriolus oriolus*

When a birdwatcher from the British Isles takes their first tentative steps into continental Europe, one of the species they long to see is the lovely golden oriole. The oriole doesn't make this easy; it is very secretive, rarely descends from the treetops and is usually only seen when it flies across a clearing or a river. What makes this worse is the glorious, liquid song, an exotic-sounding 'Weela-weeo', which makes the bird sound close and attainable, but can be heard for hours without the observer getting so much as a glimpse.

COMMON MOORHEN
Gallinula chloropus

The common moorhen is widespread in many parts of the world. It is a little ungainly, it clucks and squeals, swims with the mastery of someone swimming in treacle, and flies with amateurish incompetence.

However, when seeking out a mate, female moorhens prefer small, fat males to large, lean ones. What a very cheering thought for the day!

WOOD WARBLER
Phylloscopus sibilatrix

Above: Wood warblers are ground-nesters who breed in deciduous and mixed woods of central, east and northern Europe; winters in Africa.

Top left: The oriole summers in deciduous woods of Europe and western half of Asia; winters sub-Saharan Africa.

Bottom left: Wetlands over much of Old World except Australasia.

This brightly coloured sprite holds an astonishing secret. A summer visitor to Europe and Asia, the wood warbler arrives in April in deciduous or mixed forests to sing an effervescent, shivering song.

When most small bird species alight at their breeding grounds, they are simply looking for a territory where they can quickly settle down. Wood warblers are different. On arrival, they monitor the state of the woodland, and what they are looking for is rodents.

In northern woodlands, the populations of rodents such as voles and lemmings run on a cycle of boom and bust. If it's a bust year, the wood warblers settle in good numbers. If it's a boom year, the birds move on somewhere else. There are two reasons why. First, the rodents themselves can be nest predators of wood warblers, which nest on the ground; and second, large numbers of rodents attract an influx of predators that will also eat wood warblers.

But the bigger question is this: how on Earth does a wood warbler evaluate a rodent population? That is its great secret. Nobody knows.

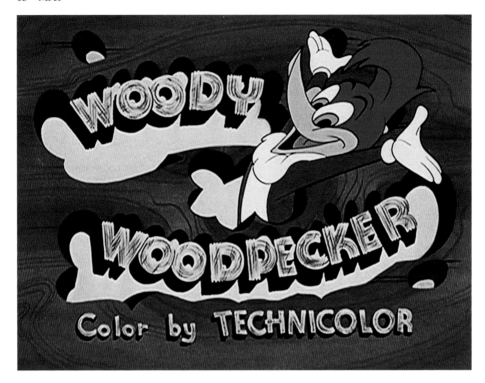

ACORN WOODPECKER
Melanerpes formicivorus

The mascot of Universal Studios is based on the acorn woodpecker, a resident of oak woodland in southern North America and Central America.

Back in the 1940s, the Hollywood producer Walter Lantz went to June Lake, California, for his honeymoon with new wife Gracie. Their bliss was apparently constantly interrupted by the calls of an acorn woodpecker, which kept them awake and, to boot, had bored holes in their cabin roof and caused it to leak. Walter Lantz was all for killing the offender, but legend has it that Gracie suggested that the bird's mischievous character be turned into a cartoon character, and this is how the much-loved Woody Woodpecker was born, the only bird with its own star on the Hollywood Walk of Fame.

Acorn woodpeckers are common birds of the south-west. Groups do indeed bore holes, often large numbers of them, in trees, in amenity poles and, no doubt, log cabins. These they use as a communal food store.

ARCTIC SKUA (ARCTIC JAEGER)
Stercorarius parasiticus

An arctic skua (bottom) mugging a kittiwake (top). This bandit breeds on coasts and tundra in northern regions of Eurasia and North America; winters in southern oceans.

Theft can be a way of life for birds, just as it can be for humans. The skuas are a small group of gull-like birds endowed with the unusual combination of webbed feet and sharp, predatory claws. They also have hook-tipped bills and pointed, falcon-like wings. This battery of armaments enables skuas not only to be predators in their own right, but also to cause trouble.

The Arctic skua, in particular, spends much of its breeding season feeding off the fishing spoils of less aggressive seabirds returning to their colonies. For example, if a kittiwake, a gentle seagoing gull, comes back to its clifftop nest, it will invariably have a crop full of fish. The Arctic skua intercepts a returnee and begins to intimidate it by flying on its tail, as if to attack. This usually has the effect of harassing the kittiwake into regurgitating its catch into the sea below. Not especially fussy, the skua picks up the spoils and will typically feed them to its own young. All it has done is use its powers of intimidation to obtain a meal with little expenditure of effort, and no injury.

143

RUBY-CROWNED KINGLET
Regulus calendula

A male ruby-crowned kinglet. Breeds in the spruce and fir forests of northern and montane North America; winters widely south to Mexico.

It is hard to look at a ruby-crowned kinglet without feeling worried for it. North America's smallest bird that isn't a hummingbird, it seems to lack the hummingbird's gumption and pizazz, with its retiring nature and vulnerable look. This, though, is an illusion. The ruby-crowned kinglet breeds right into the Arctic, can migrate long distances if the need arises, is unfussy in its winter habitat and can occupy niches that exclude most other birds. In other words, it's fine.

The kinglet breeds in stands of conifers and, unusually for most songbirds, places its nest high amidst clumps of needles – its average nest height is 12m (40ft) above ground. It lays an average of 14 eggs, which is one of the largest clutches of any songbird anywhere in the world, and it defends it fearlessly. Pretty impressive.

PIED FLYCATCHER
Ficedula hypoleuca

This little bird spends the summers in the woods of Europe and western Asia; winters in western sub-Saharan Africa.

The male pied flycatcher is a handsome love-rat. He doesn't just two-time, he has a double life. The males arrive in Eurasia in the spring, set up territories and sing. The females are soon attracted, pairs form, the female lays a clutch and all seems normal.

In the hiatus when the female is incubating, though, some males take advantage of their mate's disposition and seek another mate. What is unusual is that they don't do this within their current territory, but instead set up a completely new one, which may be 2km (1¼miles) away from the first. They attract a secondary mate and inseminate another clutch, unbeknown to their primary mate. However, as soon as the second clutch is completed, they return to the primary mate as if nothing has happened – two families, two females, none the wiser.

SAND MARTIN (BANK SWALLOW)
Riparia riparia

Sand martins are happiest nesting close together. They breed beside rivers and in sand banks across Eurasia and North America; winters in South America, Africa, south-east Asia.

The sand martin spends most of its life in the fresh air, catching insects in flight with a flick of the wings and twist of the tail. At the start of the breeding season in May, however, that changes, and the male sacrifices the outdoor life for tunnel building.

It is exhausting work, but it is the sand martin's lot to make a tunnel in the sandy substrate of riverbanks, dunes and gravel workings, for this is where he places his nest. Until he has 30cm (12in) or more of tunnel, a sand martin cannot compete for a mate.

First, he finds a projection in the vertical bank on which he can gain a foothold, then he scrapes away at the sand with his bill. When he has created a rim, the male can use his feet to kick away loose scrapings. Once he has sufficient purchase, the bill and feet continue scraping, while the wings are used to shift the bulk of the sand towards the entrance. The tunnel takes shape and, on a good day, a sand martin can burrow into the bank as much as 13cm (5in) – his own body length.

The rewards of tunnel building are high, and a bird with a good burrow soon attracts a female. Most tunnels reach at least 60cm (23½in), and some approach 1m (3¼ft) in length. And to cap it all, the male excavates a wide nesting chamber at the end.

INDIAN PARADISE FLYCATCHER

Terpsiphone paradisi

Some birds don't look real in real life, and among those are the paradise flycatchers, which are found in Africa and Asia. They are relatively common, although they look rare and exotic. Males often come in two morphs, brown and, as here, a clean, silky white. One of the highly appropriate and imaginative local Indian names for the white morph is 'cotton thief'. When flying, they do indeed look as though they are trailing some kind of fabric behind them. The tail only reaches its full length of up to 30cm (12in) when a male is two or three years old.

Indian paradise flycatchers live in woodland and forest, and often join mixed bird feeding parties. They consume large insects, including butterflies that are as spectacular as they are themselves.

Male Indian paradise flycatcher. Resident of India and Sri Lanka; summer migrant to parts of south Asia.

EASTERN SCREECH-OWL
Megascops asio

This stocky species occurs in several colour forms. Found in the woods and the gardens of eastern North America.

The soft, trilling whistle of the American-robin-sized screech owl is a familiar sound to many birders, who also use an imitation of the call to attract small birds to come out and 'mob' them. Fierce but mainly insectivorous, this beautifully camouflaged predator is often found in suburbs and city parks.

The eastern screech-owl also has a truly extraordinary habit, unknown to most people. It sometimes catches blind snakes (*Leptotyphlops dulcis*) – not for food, but for assistance in the nest hole.

Without killing them, the owls seek the snakes out and deliver them to the nest. The snakes then feast on their usual diet of ant and fly larvae and pupae. This helps the owls, because the snakes remove the pests attracted to dead prey that the owl has deliberately stored in the nest for its own young. With the insect competition removed, the owlets get more food and the nest is more likely to be successful. It's an incredibly rare example of symbiosis between snakes and birds.

BELTED KINGFISHER
Megaceryle alcyon

It's something of a myth that everything is bigger in America, but in the case of kingfishers, it's certainly true. The belted kingfisher is 28–35cm (11–14in) long, compared with the common kingfisher, which is only 16cm (around 6in) long – half the size. The belted also dives from a greater height than the common kingfisher. Moreover, common kingfishers usually dig a tunnel about 1m (3¼ft) long, but belted tunnels often reach 2m (6½ft) in length and, remarkably, over 6m (over 19½ft) has been recorded.

BEE HUMMINGBIRD
Mellisuga helenae

Here's a thought for the day to celebrate the wondrous diversity of birds: the ostrich's eye is the same size as the world's smallest bird, the bee hummingbird. This midget is 5–6cm (about 2in) long, and while an ostrich eye weighs 47.6g (1²/₃oz), the male bee hummingbird weighs as little as 1.6g (¹/₂₀oz).

The bee hummingbird is rare, being found only in Cuba.

Above: This North American species holds the record for most songs in one day. It winters in Central America and northern South America.

Top left: Wetlands across North America; summer visitor to north, and winters down to northern South America.

Bottom left: Breeding now in flowery places in parts of Cuba and Isla de la Juventud.

RED-EYED VIREO
Vireo olivaceus

On this May day in Canada in 1952, a Swedish-born ornithologist Louise de Kiriline Lawrence was challenged by a friend to do a 'Big Day', usually devoted to seeing as many species as possible in a 24-hour period. Lawrence decided to do something different: to count the number of songs her local red-eyed vireo sang in a day. This was a challenge, because these birds have short, cheery phrases which, in the peak of the breeding season, are sung incessantly.

When the vireo had sung 1,700 songs by 5am, Lawrence must have been tempted to stop counting. But she didn't, and by nightfall the bird had completed 22,197 songs, give or take a few. That was one very persistent singing bird, and a very persistent ornithologist.

ROSE-RINGED PARAKEET
Psittacula krameri

A resident of multicultural London, this bird is actually native to woods of the Sahel belt of the Indian subcontinent and Africa.

Bright grass-green, apart from a red bill and eyes and a collar of black, rose and lilac around its neck, the rose-ringed parakeet is everyone's idea of a middle-of-the-road parrot, with a voice to match – a persistent screech that isn't easy on the ear. You would not pick this parakeet out as exceptional.

Except that it is. In the wild state it is one of the few birds that flourishes both in Africa and India. In the latter it has adapted to the cold climate of the Himalayan foothills, which is also unusual for a warmth-loving parrot. In lowland India it is by far the most common species, with roosts of many thousands in cities such as Delhi, and in rural areas it can be a serious pest to crops.

Its abundance led to a second career as a popular cage bird, which continues on a massive scale. And this, inadvertently, has now given the bird a third career as an invasive species. Releases, intentional and otherwise, have meant that the rose-ringed parakeet now flourishes in 34 countries on five continents. These include such incongruous places as the UK, with its chilly, damp climate and Belgium, where it occupies the urban fringe.

In Britain, the rumour-mill has long suggested that the population stems from the release of a pair by the guitarist Jimi Hendrix in Carnaby Street, London, in the 1960s, but of course this isn't true!

YELLOW-BILLED CHOUGH
Pyrrhocorax graculus

Above: A bird of the high places – the mountains of Eurasia and North Africa.

Top right: This fussy bird summers in jack pine forests around the Great Lakes; winters in the Bahamas.

Bottom right: Resident of freshwater marshes, lakes and swamp forests of South and Central America, the Caribbean and Florida.

It was on this day in 1953 that New Zealander Sir Edmund Hillary and Sherpa Tenzing Norgay (originally from Nepal) made the first successful ascent of the world's tallest land mountain, Mount Everest, putting the first human feet on the 8,848m (29,029ft) summit.

There's little doubt that they were well beaten to it by a bird. The alpine chough is the ultimate high-altitude species, almost never seen below 1,500m (5,000ft) in Eurasia. It occurs in the Himalayas and has been seen by climbers as high as 8,235m (27,000ft). It can even breed in caves at 5,000m (16,400ft).

KIRTLAND'S WARBLER
Setophaga kirtlandii

Found breeding only in parts of Michigan, Wisconsin and a sliver of southern Ontario, Kirtland's Warbler is one of the North America's scarcest gems. It must always have been rare, because it is astonishingly fussy. It only breeds in one kind of woodland, that of the jack pine (*Pinus banksiana*). The trees have to be dense and young, 5–23 years old, and they must be on sandy soils on glacial outwash. The trees must be 1.2–5m(4–16½ft) tall with live lower branches. Apart from that, the bird can occur everywhere.

LIMPKIN
Aramus guarauna

The Limpkin is an odd bird of marshes in the Americas. Perhaps the oddest thing about the Limpkin is its diet, which consists of nothing but molluscs. Its eats freshwater mussels, but its favourite nourishment is snails, which can comprise 100% of the diet in some areas. To open large snails, it lodges them on a surface, aperture facing up, holds on to them with the toes of one leg, and uses the bill to break the snail's protective operculum, then cut the muscles holding the animal in its shell.

MARSH WARBLER
Acrocephalus palustris

Above: Thickets and shrubbery in Europe; winters in extreme south-east Africa.

Top right: 'Sings' in prairies and grasslands of northeast USA; winters on the Atlantic and Gulf coasts.

Bottom right: A rare example of this extint bird, which once inhabited the islands and coasts of the North Atlantic, for sale at Sotheby's in 1977..

Over much of Europe the plain-coloured marsh warbler is only now arriving at its breeding grounds and establishing territories, the latest summer visitor to do so. The song, though, is worth waiting for, a fast-paced, wacky tangle of song fragments seemingly delivered at random – rap music from a bird, perhaps.

The song is amazing. Although the delivery is the bird's own, the elements are almost all from other birds, which the male marsh warbler deftly copies.

A wonderful study among a group of birds in Belgium, showed that the marsh warbler learns its song during its first year, which includes its migration to tropical Africa. Intermixed in the delivery are bird calls from Europe and Africa: a sparrow followed by a weaver bird; or a sunbird followed by a tit. The study found more than 200 species copied in a population of Belgian birds, half of them from Africa.

HENSLOW'S SPARROW
Centronyx henslowii

It is hard not to smile when watching the Henslow's sparrow sing. This bird of North American grassland has one of the least impressive of all bird songs. It has been described as a feeble hiccup. It goes 'Tsip', and that's it. What is amusing is the performance that goes into this pathetic refrain. The bird makes his way to the top of a stem, opens his mouth wide, throws his head back like an opera singer mid-aria, and the result falls hilariously flat. The females, presumably, give marks for effort.

GREAT AUK
Pinguinus impennis

This day in 1844 was one of small-scale, everyday savagery. A group of fishermen landed on the island of Eldey, off Iceland, commissioned with the task of acquiring specimens of the increasingly rare great auk. They came across just a single pair, attending an egg. The men strangled the two adults and smashed the egg on the rocks. No breeding pair of great auks was ever seen again; indeed, the bird was only seen alive once more, off Newfoundland in December 1852.

HIMALAYAN MONAL
Lophophorus impejanus

You might expect the world's highest mountains to hide something special, and the jewels of the Himalayan crown are a glittering array of members of the pheasant family. The Himalayan monal occurs in mixed forest and meadows at altitudes between 2,400m and 4,500m (7,800 and 14,800ft). It is just one of a number of truly spectacular species with heavily bejewelled feathered bling. It would be worth the climb to see one of these beauties.

HOUSE FINCH
Haemorhous mexicanus

One of the most familiar birds of North America, the house finch is found almost everywhere, from deserts to the centre of cities. It has a pleasant, highly variable warbling song.

It is a bird that has had to adapt to singing in places with noisy human activity. In Mexico City, individuals from busy neighbourhoods sing higher-pitched songs than birds from quieter places, so that they can be heard above the human hubbub.

SPRAGUE'S PIPIT
Anthus spragueii

Above: This pipit breeds in short-grass prairies in midwest; winters Texas to Mexico.

Top left: Mixed forests and meadows of Himalayan region.

Bottom left: Resident and common across many habitats in North America, from Canadian border south to Mexico.

Look at the Sprague's pipit and you will not be excited; it is the epitome of a small, streaky brown bird. Listen to the Sprague's pipit and, again, there's nothing that will get the juices flowing. It utters a dull, dry series of whistles; its song is nobody's favourite tune.

But what this bird lacks in charisma it makes up for in stamina. When males sing in the spring and early summer, they spiral up to 100m (330ft) or more above the North American prairies where they breed, and just stay aloft. It is rare for any songbird to perform for more than a few minutes aloft, but these birds are famed for the indefatigability. Males have often been observed song-flighting for an hour – and even up to three hours – non-stop. That could be a world record.

BROWN THRASHER
Toxostoma rufum

This fearless bird favours woods and thickets in the eastern half of North America; summer visitor in midwest and north of the Carolinas.

Common but not completely familiar owing to its retiring habits and avoidance of the backyard scrum, the brown thrasher could be considered a curious state emblem. Nevertheless, it has been adopted by Georgia, and one of its attributes, for which it has long been famous after being painted by American naturalist John James Audubon in the process of protecting its nest from snakes (shown above), is its remarkable courage. Thrashers will not relent in their staunch nest defence and must sometimes be killed while doing so.

Snakes are common nest predators, and brown thrashers have been reliably reported attacking at least three species. They use their long, sharp bills to peck towards the reptiles' eyes, and it is rumoured that they sometimes pluck out eyes. They can certainly draw blood.

Other objects of the thrashers' ire may be humans, if they draw too close. It is advisable not to provoke them!

COMMON KINGFISHER
Alcedo atthis

There is nothing common about this bird of streams and rivers across Europe and Asia, North Africa and Indonesia.

There are many reasons to adore the kingfisher. Its dazzling plumage is scintillating, it has an attractive habit of bobbing up and down on perches, and who isn't thrilled to see one plunge-dive into shallow water to snare a small fish?

A much less well-known reason to love kingfishers is the marvellous, democratic way in which they feed their nestlings in the early stages. The young sit in a circle in the nesting chamber with their backs to one another, looking outwards. One chick faces the light that comes in from the tunnel entrance. When the adult arrives with a fish, this chick takes the offering. Then, all the chicks move round until the next bird on the carousel is facing the light, and is in position to take the next meal.

This is a rare example of co-operation among nestlings.

COMMON EIDER
Somateria mollissima

The female eider has camouflaging feathers but the male is a distinctive black and white in the breeding season. They live on rocky coasts of northern Eurasia and North America.

The down of the eider duck is known the world over. The feathers covering this northern and Arctic duck have the most perfect insulating properties in the world, so much so that they have created a small industry for luxury bedding. No synthetic material has ever come close to providing the softness and warmth of eider down: it is possible to have a comfortable night in a sleeping bag even when it is a blood-curdling -31°C (-23.8°F) outside.

The feathers come from the breast of the female, who often doesn't move at all during the incubation period of 26 days, except to take a drink every few days.

Even today, a few people still make a living taking the down from colonies of eiders, mostly in Iceland. The down is harvested twice, at the beginning and end of the incubation period. These days a real eider-down duvet will cost in excess of $5,000.

FIELDFARE
Turdus pilaris

Don't mess
with a fieldfare
(here fighting
a common
blackbird) or
the mess will
be on you. The
bird breeds in
woodland, scrub
and gardens in
Eurasia; some
winter south
as far as North
Africa and
Middle East.

Birds have evolved many ways of defending their nests, but one of the most remarkable is the method employed by a common Eurasian thrush, the fieldfare.

Fieldfares nest in loose colonies, with nests about 10m (33ft) apart, enough for birds to be in close contact with one another. At the egg and nestling stage, pairs can be extremely aggressive towards predators, especially other birds such as crows, owls or raptors, and are able to co-ordinate their attacks if an intruder appears.

The form of attack is extraordinary. The fieldfares fly up over the miscreant visitor, then dive down on it from above, ejecting a missile of excreta as they do so. One bird defecates, followed by another and another, until the unfortunate predator, if it stays put, becomes spattered with excrement. Quite apart from being unpleasant, this could cause the plumage to become matted and compromised, and even prove fatal.

163

Above: These birds prefer the warm regions of Europe and west Asia with winters sub-Saharan Africa.

Top right: This North American woodland thrush winters in Central America.

Bottom right: In summer these martins favour man-made American houses but winters in lowland South America south to Brazil.

EUROPEAN BEE-EATER
Merops apiaster

Is the European bee-eater the perfect bird? Stunning with its bright coloration, and effortlessly graceful in flight, the bee-eater even has a liquid call that's easy on the ear. Breeding in kaleidoscopic colonies, usually in areas of warm sunshine, it is unsurprisingly a favourite among birdwatchers. What isn't to like? Back in the 4th century BCE the father of natural history, the Greek polymath Aristotle, was familiar with the bird and wrote some extraordinary detail about it. He knew, for example, that youngsters will sometimes help the adults feed their young in the nest. It took the best part of 2,000 years for that to be confirmed by scientists.

In truth, bee-eaters are not universally loved, because they are consumers of bees and other flying insects, making them an enemy of the apiarist. The birds can consume more than 200 bees a day, and in the past the birds have been persecuted, and sometimes eaten into the bargain.

WOOD THRUSH
Hylocichla mustelina

In the turbulence of life, many people turn to therapy. For some, a simpler cure might be to listen to a wood thrush singing for a few minutes each day. The loveliness of this thrush's song lies in its reassuring tones and haunting melodies; listen for a while and time stands still.

Regrettably, although still numerous in forests and woodland in the east of North America, wood thrush populations are declining alarmingly.

The world needs birds like this.

PURPLE MARTIN
Progne subis

The purple martin is one of North America's most popular birds. Until recently there were three national organizations dedicated to its welfare. It has its own quarterly magazine, and there are thousands of places you can buy purple martin boxes. The devotion to this bird has lasted for more than 100 years.

Interestingly, in Mexico and parts of the west, purple martins nest in holes in trees instead, forsaking boxes completely. They also nest singly.

ATLANTIC PUFFIN
Fratercula arctica

The puffin breeds on islands and coasts around the North Atlantic, including the UK, and deep into the Arctic; winters at sea.

The 'clown of the seas', the Atlantic puffin is many people's favourite sea bird, with its colourful beak, upright posture and waddling gait. It breeds by Atlantic coasts, often on islands, digging a burrow in the turf at the clifftop, or finding a hole in the cliff itself. The window of opportunity for seeing them is short; between April and July the birds are at their burrows, but the rest of the year they spend out at sea, often above the deep ocean.

Another reason everybody loves puffins is that, when they arrive at a nest hole to feed their young, they carry fish horizontally in their bill. They usually collect 6–8 at a time, but birds have been recorded carrying more – as many as 62 have been counted. Small, backward projections in its colourful beak, plus the tongue, help the puffin hold on to this mouthful.

WESTERN MEADOWLARK
Sturnella neglecta

Nothing conveys the atmosphere of the open prairies, fields and meadows of the American West more perfectly than the glorious fluty, crystal-clear song of the western meadowlark. It can be heard for most of the summer, from March to August, and also sporadically in winter. It is usually given from a low perch, such as a fence post, and is a song that should ideally be heard on a calm, warm day with the sun in your back.

The western meadowlark has a song distinct from its counterpart the eastern meadowlark (*S. magna*). The birds are almost identical in appearance, but their songs are enough to keep them apart. The song of a male western meadowlark will stop an eastern meadowlark from entering its territory – a rare example of a song of one species excluding another.

A meadowlark of the western half of North America; winters south to Mexico.

ISLE OF MAN   28

Dr. Jeremy Paul   The Agency Design   2006   Cartor

MANX SHEARWATER
Puffinus puffinus

Breeding now on offshore islands of the North Atlantic, mainly Europe; migrates to South Atlantic.

In 1952 a breeding Manx shearwater from the small Welsh Island of Skokholm was taken by plane to Boston, Massachusetts, and released at the airport. It immediately orientated itself and began to fly back towards its burrow; it arrived there on 16 June, 12½ days later, having flown a distance of more than 5,000km (3,000 miles) at a rate of about 400km (250 miles) a day. In fact, the bird arrived before the letter announcing its release in Boston was received back in Wales! This was early proof of the extraordinary ability of birds to navigate, something that still isn't fully understood today.

EUROPEAN NIGHTJAR
Caprimulgus europaeus

Heard now in open country, woodland edge and heath across Europe and west Asia; winters in sub-Saharan Africa.

It's deep summer in the northern hemisphere. However long the days might be, we still wish they could last longer, and the fullness never fade.

The nights are sweet, too, though, short and balmy and more mysterious than winter nights, with more possibility. These are the nights to listen for one of nature's oddest sounds, the 'churring' of the nightjar.

This nocturnal bird – perhaps more a twilight bird – takes advantage of the poorly recognized bloom of night-flying insects that fills the crepuscular skies – moths, beetles, caddisflies and the like. It sweeps the airspace, spotting small bodies against the sky and trapping them in its outsize gape.

And then, when not feeding, the male makes its bizarre advertising call, a hollow trill that shifts between two tones, like a two-stroke motorcycle. Coming from the shadows, it is eerie and unearthly, a spirit of the night. To hear one under a fair-season, starry sky is unforgettable.

HOOPOE
Upupa epops

The hoopoe is common in open woodland and gardens in many warm regions of the Old World.

The exotic-looking hoopoe is a great favourite of birdwatchers, occurring in Europe, Africa and large parts of Asia. After all, not many birds are salmon-pink, with an outrageous crest.

Good looks aside, the hoopoe is also famously unhygienic. Not only does it probe into dung heaps (for insects) with alacrity, but the nest is legendarily odorous, because both female and young produce a defensive, foul-smelling extrusion from their preen gland. Furthermore, young hoopoes can eject disgusting pellets of faeces at an intruder with remarkable accuracy. They can hit you even when you're 60cm (24in) away! So be warned – don't get too close.

LAYSAN DUCK
Anas laysanensis

Teetering on the
brink in Hawaii.

It is possible that no single bird species has flirted with extinction like the Laysan duck, a bird confined to its eponymous island, a tiny atoll in the Hawaiian archipelago just 370ha (914 acres) in extent and separated from the nearest island by 500km (300 miles) of ocean. The ducks relied on eating brine shrimps from the island's lake.

Owing to the depredations of guano mining, hunting and the introduction of rabbits, in 1930 the population was down to about seven birds, of which only one was a female. Mercifully, that year the female laid a clutch of eggs. Disaster struck, though, when another rare bird, the bristle-thighed curlew, raided the nest and destroyed the eggs.

Miraculously, that same female relaid a clutch and this time the chicks survived, including some females. By this time the miners had left, the rabbits had starved, and the population gradually recovered. There are now about 500 birds.

ROSEATE SPOONBILL
Platalea ajaja

Wetlands of South America, then mainly coastal Central America north to Texas and Florida.

If the roseate spoonbill didn't exist, a child would probably have invented it in their imagination – drawing a bird with a strange bill and using a bright crayon to fill it in with improbable pink. Nothing quite prepares you for the sight of a real one flying past, its neck stretched out, legs trailing and stiff wingbeats interspersed with gliding, a pink marvel.

The roseate spoonbill feeds in shallow fresh or saline water in a distinctive way, wading deep and sweeping its slightly opened bill rapidly from side to side. When the bill touches an edible item, such as a fish, crustacean or insect larva, it snaps shut at incredible speed. All prey is caught in its famous 'spoon'.

SPOTTED SANDPIPER
Actitis macularius

The distinctive egg of a spotted sandpiper. They are breeding near water at the moment across northern half of North America, and winter from south USA to Argentina.

If you happen to have heard the term 'rapid multi-clutching', you may well have assumed it referred to something mechanical relating to cars. In fact, it describes the breeding behaviour of some shorebirds.

The spotted sandpiper is a definitive example. At its heart, multi-clutching is just that, laying multiple clutches of eggs in a single season. A female of this species in Minnesota, USA, once laid five clutches in 43 days (usually of four eggs). In order for the system to work, though, a female must subcontract incubation duties to the male – or indeed, several males.

And that's what happens. A female produces a clutch, hands it over to the male to incubate, moves on to mate with a second male, lays a clutch, leaves it with partner number two, and so on. Some spotted sandpipers have been known to pair with four males in one summer.

BUDGERIGAR
Melopsittacus undulatus

In the wild, in their native Australia, budgies belong to nomadic flocks. They stick to arid and semi-arid areas with some trees.

The budgerigar has been a popular cage bird since the 1850s, and as such is familiar to most of us. It is easy to keep in captivity, eating little but grain and readily breeding if a nest box is provided. Its cheery, soft calls are pleasing on the ear, and it can be taught to say human words. A famous budgie in the United States was able to reproduce 1,777 human words or phrases.

Its domestic life is a far cry from its life in the wild in the arid areas of Australia. This isn't a bird you can expect to see easily on a short visit, in contrast to ubiquitous icons such as kangaroos and kookaburras. In the Outback it is highly nomadic, materializing in places seemingly at random, chasing the production of grass seeds after rains. The birds use holes in trees for their nests. In dry years, large flocks may gather at waterholes, sometimes wheeling and darting like flocks of locusts. The budgerigar is well-adapted to harsh conditions, often barely drinking at all on a given day.

You could argue that, in captivity, we just don't see the real budgie. And in fact, the same applies to its appearance. The cheek spots have a very high UV reflectance, and the yellow cheek and crown are fluorescent, so what a budgerigar sees in another budgerigar is quite different to what we are able to perceive.

AFRICAN GREY PARROT
Psittacus erithacus

A good many birds can be taught to talk, mynahs and budgerigars among them. The African grey parrot can be taught not just to talk, but to communicate. This was proved in a series of experiments carried out by Dr Irene Pepperberg, from the 1970s to the 2000s. She performed tests on a bird called Alex and discovered that he was capable of counting, understanding concepts and reasoning. He had a vocabulary of over 100 words but, rather than using them at random, could name objects such as food items. He could understand and communicate the difference between big and small, and whether things were the same or different. He could express emotions such as anger and would ask to return to his cage when he became tired of the tests.

This remarkable individual was estimated to have the language skills of a two-year-old human child, and the cognitive intelligence of a five-year-old human or a great ape such as a chimpanzee.

YELLOWHAMMER
Emberiza citrinella

Pity the male yellowhammer. On long summer days in northern Europe, when it feels too hot to exhale, let alone sing, this popular hedgerow bird may utter its dry ditty 3,000 times a day. And even then, its attempts at 'A little bit of bread and no cheeeeeese' may not be deemed adequate by a potential mate. Females also closely monitor just how colourfully pigmented a bird is in the red and yellow spectrum. If it's not intense enough, he is not good enough. Making the grade is tough!

WHITE-THROATED SPARROW
Zonotrichia albicollis

The white-throated sparrow shows an extraordinary plumage quirk, almost unique among birds. Individuals of both sexes come in two forms, white-striped (clean white markings on the head and throat) and tan-striped (markings less obvious and tinged with grey). Male white-striped individuals sing more often and are more aggressive than tan-striped males, but individuals will almost invariably mate with a member of the opposite morph.

EUROPEAN HERRING GULL
Larus argentatus

These flying desperadoes are well-known on many coasts and wetlands of north-eastern Atlantic and Baltic region.

Herring gulls are the loud ones whose clanging calls are so much a part of the atmosphere of northern European seaside towns. They are large, assertive birds, and it seems that this assertiveness begins early in life.

The gulls nest in densely packed colonies on the ground, sometimes on cliffs. Neighbours constantly bicker as there isn't much space between nests. And woe betide any young, fluffy gull that has only recently hatched, and wanders by mistake from its nest: it is likely to be pecked to death by territorial adults.

This aggressive neighbourhood is the youngster's home from the time it hatches until it is a month old. Relief is provided by the many visits made by its parents, which regurgitate regular meals. The youngsters grow quickly.

Except occasionally, they don't. Some parents are useless, and don't bring enough food. The chicks grow hungrier and hungrier, until they are on the point of starvation, at which point they may make the most extraordinary decision. They jump ship to any neighbouring territory where the parents are more competent – they fire their own parents.

It's a terrible risk and it often proves fatal, but from time to time chicks are accepted and fed by neighbouring pairs. To be honest, the chicks don't have a lot of choice. They are likely to die from inadequate parenting or from being attacked by neighbours, so they have little to lose.

COMMON QUAIL

Coturnix coturnix

The common quail is a mysterious species. It is common in Europe in the summer, but almost never seen. Its distinctive 'Wet-me-lips' call can come virtually from your feet and you'll never see the bird. Until very recently, almost all the details about its breeding habits were unknown. We now know that it can breed in northern Africa in March, and then both adults and young can undertake a second migration in mid-summer, and those three-month old youngsters will breed too.

Early accounts of quails also give us a tantalising glimpse of what birdwatching might have been like in ancient times. There are Egyptian wall paintings depicting people hunting quail in fields, the birds themselves illustrated with remarkable accuracy. There are accounts from Pliny about quails landing on boats in such numbers as they sank them. And in the Bible, quails were the meat that God gave the Israelites in the wilderness. The account in Numbers 11, 31–34 begins: 'And there went forth a wind from the Lord and brought quails from the sea, and let them fall by the camp ... And the people stood up all that day, and all that night and all the next day, and they gathered the quails ...'

Even today people sometimes experience hundreds or thousands of quail migrating by night, especially in Egypt, where they are netted in large numbers. But how marvellous must have been the abundance of birds in ancient times when man's footprint was still fairly light on the Earth.

This piece, in the British Museum, London, shows Nebumun out hunting birds, including quail. Today, quail can be found in fields and grasslands of much of Eurasia; they winter in India and Africa, with some resident in the latter.

PURPLE SANDPIPER
Calidris maritima

Breeds in the Arctic tundra of Greenland, Canada and Eurasia; winters along rocky coasts well to the south.

The purple sandpiper is a shorebird that breeds on tundra and beaches in the High Arctic – and does something truly amazing.

This far north the nest must go on the ground because there are no trees, so it is very vulnerable. Both parents go to extreme measures to protect the eggs and young. Their most remarkable anti-predator technique is an extraordinary form of deception. Believe it or not, they pretend to be tasty rodents.

It's true. As a predator approaches, the purple sandpiper crouches (with only the lower part of its leg showing), ruffles its feathers, quivers its wings and squeals like a mouse. Since most Arctic predators are always on the lookout for voles or lemmings, they will chase after it. The sandpiper may lead the intruder as far as 500m (almost ⅓ mile) from the nest, and then fly off, leaving the predator highly confused but with the eggs or chicks still safely in the nest.

WILSON'S STORM-PETREL
Oceanites oceanicus

Storm petrel, apparently running on water. They breed on islands in the Atlantic, Pacific and Indian Oceans, wandering far in non-breeding season.

Today is St Peter's Day, celebrated in honour of the disciple who briefly walked on the water to try to reach Jesus. It remembers those who risk their lives on the sea.

The English name 'petrel' derives from 'Peter'. It is highly appropriate, since these minute sea birds regularly patter their yellow feet on the surface of the water while they are flying just above the waves. These birds feed on small planktonic animals.

SATIN BOWERBIRD
Ptilonorhynchus violaceus

Collectors of unconsidered blue trifles in the rainforest and wet eucalypt forests of south-eastern Australia.

Y ou could never accuse a male satin bowerbird of not trying hard to please the women in his life. And you couldn't possibly accuse a female satin bowerbird of making it easy. The female is arguably the choosiest of any species in the world.

The bowerbirds are famous, as their name implies, for making 'bowers'. These are structures that have no practical benefit – they aren't nests or roost sites, nor are they useful as feeding sites. They are made by males purely to attract females, who can then assess the quality of the builder.

The male satin bowerbirds put in enormous efforts to construct and decorate their bower. They build two walls of sticks with a gap in between, the 'avenue' between two screens. The walls may contain more than 2,000 carefully gathered sticks. For decoration the builders then collect a large number of miscellaneous items (more than 300), which may include stones, skulls, seeds and feathers and, in urban fringes (for example near Sydney or Canberra), sweet packets, matchboxes, envelopes, string and glass. The most highly prized items are blue. Even the corpse of a fairywren, an electric blue midget, has been found in a bower. Amazingly, the male even paints some items, using its bill to plaster masticated plant products on them – all in the name of artistic construction.

No matter how opulent the bower, when a female arrives, the male also has to sing and display. For a female, there are plenty of males to visit. Only a tiny minority are successful in persuading an impressed visitor to mate.

GREAT NORTHERN DIVER (COMMON LOON)
Gavia immer

Above: Loons breed in northern North America and Iceland on lakes; winter in shallow seas off both coasts, and northern Europe.

Top right: Breeds in a few colonies in Antarctic about now.

Bottom right: This livestock groupie lives throughout the warmer regions of the world.

Today is Canada Day and it seems as if there is a pair of common loons on every Canadian lake, small or large, so it is appropriate that this is the country's national bird, with the $1 coin popularly called a Loony. A hardy, northern bird that chases fish underwater, the loon is characteristic of the vastness of the forest-lake taiga of North America. Here, every spring, common loons utter their unforgettable laughing calls, day or night. There is a scintilla of menace in the sound, which means that it is part of many a movie soundtrack to conjure a fear of the wild.

Powerful in flight, at ease underwater, the common loon has long been used by shamans of northern regions as a passage to another world, the human subconscious represented by the watery depths.

EMPEROR PENGUIN
Aptenodytes forsteri

At this time of year, the Antarctic winter is raging. In a fit of adaptive madness, emperor penguins are on the ice sheets, incubating their eggs where no potential predator would dare to go. The male penguins, eggs resting on their feet, may be huddled together facing the brunt of a violent storm, with winds over 120km/h (75mph) and a temperature of -60°C (-76°).

By contrast, on the same day at the equator, Galapagos penguins could be incubating their eggs in searing heat of up to 40°C (104°F).

CATTLE EGRET
Bubulcus ibis

The cattle egret might be related to herons and egrets, but it doesn't act like one. Largely eschewing fishing duties near water, instead it seeks out the nearest large grazing animals, such as cattle, even elephants and rhinos, and forages next to them, sometimes standing on their backs. The egrets don't usually take food directly from the mammals' hide, but instead use the animals as lookouts, and jump down to pick up invertebrates disturbed by the animals' feet.

BALD EAGLE
Haliaeetus leucocephalus

Resident: A keen fisherman, the bald eagle loves the coasts and wetlands of North America; it winters widely, down to the Mexican border.

The magnificent bald eagle was adopted as the national bird of the USA back in 1782. Huge, with broad wings and, in adults, a smart, all-white head and tail, it has long represented power and freedom, even well back in the history of indigenous communities. There is indeed much to admire in this bird: its good looks, strength, and awesome flight display, in which pairs lock talons high in the air and then cartwheel downwards at great speed, only stopping when they have almost reached the ground.

In common with all icons, however, bald eagles aren't universally admirable. They frequently steal food from each other. They have a tendency to be lazy, seeking carrion rather than bothering to catch live food. And while it is proverbial for eagles to be masters of the air, catching fast-moving prey, bald eagles are usually perfectly satisfied with fish.

CORN BUNTING
Emberiza calandra

The corn bunting of lowland Europe, North Africa and west Asia, has plenty to sing about.

It's plump, it's plain and to us it has little to recommend it. Its courtship display involves nothing more than flying from perch to perch with its legs dangling – big deal. However, the song of the corn bunting sounds like the jangling of a set of keys and is one of the most familiar and persistent songs among European birds, lasting deep into the summer, when most birds have stopped.

With no looks and no charisma, you'd think the corn bunting's sex life would be dull. Consider this then. Dominant male corn buntings often mate with several females; one bird in southern England mated with 18 females in one season!

189

CALLIOPE HUMMINGBIRD
Selasphorus calliope

Found in meadows and riverside thickets in the Rocky Mountains this little powerhouse migrates south to Mexico.

North America's smallest bird is extraordinary. At a mere 7.5–8cm (3in) in length, and weighing only 2.6g ($^1/_{10}$oz), it is among the tinier hummingbirds. Yet it defies its physical limitations to live in montane forests as far north as British Columbia, where the nights are often cold, even in summer. And then, at the end of the season, it undergoes a remarkable migration to Mexico, taking it as far as 3,900km (2,400 miles) to the south. It takes a longer route north in spring, amounting to 5,400km (3,350 miles), meaning that it can fly about 9,300km (5,800 miles) in a year. It is, indeed, the smallest long-distance migrant in the world.

WOOD STORK
Mycteria americana

In case you are reading this on a hot day, some advice for cooling down the body follows, as practiced by the wood stork. All you do is urinate on yourself. The process of evaporation cools the blood vessels in the legs, and the chilled blood will then circulate around the rest of the body.

It might help to perch high in a tree first.

This stork favours ponds and wetlands with large fish from Florida and Mexico south to northern Argentina.

SNOW BUNTING
Plectrophenax nivalis

This hardy bird breeds in tundra in Arctic and Boreal regions; winters south on fields and plains.

Breeding further north than any other songbird in the world, the snow bunting flourishes in places where you and I would quickly perish. It can cope with temperatures of -30°C (-22°F), although if the cold plunges to -50°C (-58°F) that can rapidly be fatal.

Snow buntings have thick feathers and they frequently crouch to nestle their partially feathered legs among the plumage of their belly. In dangerous conditions they can also dig into the snow to make a hollow, where they can sit out stormy nights and days.

In the summer breeding season, migrant males arrive up to six weeks before the females in the High Arctic. There is much competition for nest sites, which are in deep holes in rocks. The best sites are the warmest and most sheltered. Some birds have taken to using unusual sites – inside the skull of a dead animal is a popular choice.

AMERICAN GOLDFINCH
Spinus tristis

An American goldfinch nest has a snug interior about 6.5cm (2½in) in diameter. It can be found in fields, hedges and overgrown gardens across North America.

It's early July and summer has settled in. Most songbirds of northern latitudes are well underway with breeding, with a brood to feed or even the first one done and dusted. Some may be sighing with relief that reproduction is nearly over for the year.

Not, so the American goldfinch, the last songbird of that continent to get going. It doesn't even start building a nest until now and second broods continue well into August. It is thought that nest-building is stimulated by the appearance of thistledown for nesting and seeds for feeding young, which happens beyond mid-summer. Fewer nest-raiding predators are around, too.

The nest itself is wondrous. It takes the female a week to build. It is a cup with a base of spider silk, covered by a layer of rootlets and, finally, a layer of thistledown. It is so skilfully made that an empty nest can hold water after rain.

ANDEAN COCK-OF-THE-ROCK
Rupicola peruvianus

The national bird of Peru lives in montane forest in the northern Andes, south to Bolivia.

Imagine turning a corner in a South American montane forest and coming across this. The male Andean cock-of-the-rock is one of life's lookers, endowed with rich crimson plumage and a curly fringe. The male spends much of its life displaying, its fruit diet being easy to find.

Male cocks-of-the-rock don't display alone, but in groups of up to 15, in a gathering known as a lek. The principle behind a lek is that, as males display among themselves, one bird proves its dominance. When a female visits, she will find and mate only with the dominant bird, the rest of the males being ignored.

Remarkably, when a female appears, male cocks-of-the-rock display in pairs or trios, facing one another a few metres apart, bowing, jumping, wing-flapping, and making grunting and squawking calls. The overall display is thus a combined effort, but still only one male will get the female's attention.

NORTHERN FULMAR
Fulmarus glacialis

This abundant bird nests on islands and cliffs across northern seas, especially the Atlantic and Arctic Ocean; local north Pacific Ocean.

Here's a claim to fame – the fulmar is 'celebrated' for its vomiting habit. If the adults or young are threatened on the nest, they expel a foul-smelling, warm, yellowish goo that is unerringly aimed at the intruder. The birds tend to shoot first rather than negotiating, which means that entirely innocent researchers are regularly covered in a potion that can remain revolting for literally years afterwards.

This hasn't always deterred the North Atlantic islanders, for example those on the Faeroes, from harvesting adult fulmars and their eggs. They still take about 100,000 annually, even for a bird that is decidedly an acquired taste.

VILLAGE WEAVER
Ploceus cucullatus

Justly famous for its nests, this bird can be found in savanna, fields and gardens throughout much of sub-Saharan Africa, except the far south-west.

No visitor to the bush or wildlife parks of sub-Saharan Africa could possibly miss the amazing nests of weavers, or 'weaver-birds'. Many a tree in open country is adorned with masses of these globular structures, which are the equivalent of high-rise tenement blocks. There are many species of weavers, and they all make intricately woven nests, many, like those of the village weaver, in conspicuous colonies.

The nests are made by the males, initially to attract females, and each male constructs several nests within its own personal corner of a tree. Weaving a nest from strands of green grass using only the bill is highly skilled, and some males are simply better than others. They use various types of knots, including 'half-hitching' and slip-knots. Sooner or later a female will visit to inspect the interior, a process that can take 20 minutes. If she likes it, she will mate with the male and line it – completing the interior, you might say. The nest now assumes its main purpose: becoming a place to raise the young.

CRESTED AUKLET
Aethia cristatella

Found on remote
coastlines and
islands of the
Bering Strait;
winters out at sea.

The crested auklet is a tiny sea bird, related to the puffin, which breeds in large colonies on islands in the Bering Sea off the coasts of Russia and Alaska. It has a very odd claim to fame – an extreme case of body odour. Both males and females give off a pungent smell which is apparently closest to tangerine – at any rate, a citrus.

The smell is such that you can tell you are nearing a colony simply by catching the scent downwind, and it can carry for 10km (over 6 miles). In theory you could add this bird to a list of species you've encountered without either hearing or seeing it.

The smell is thought to be a form of communication; it could be that the birds recognize their natal colonies by their distinctive odour.

COMMON SHELDUCK
Tadorna tadorna

Found on sandy and muddy coasts and steppe lakes from western Europe to central Asia; winters further south.

It's mid-July and the shelducks of Europe are gathering for a strange kind of 'festival'. Thousands have travelled to the vast mud banks of the Wadden Sea, off the coast of Denmark and Germany. Almost the entire European breeding population, at least 100,000 birds, finds safety on the treacherous flats, far away from even the most reckless of four-footed predators.

They come here because, for a couple of weeks in late July, shelducks lose their flight feathers practically all at once, and their ability to take off becomes impaired or interrupted altogether. Their safety is compromised to the extent that they take the trouble first to fly to this special spot, even from over 1,000km (620 miles) away.

It is an astonishing example of a special 'moult migration'. They will return in a few months, after a summer of eating well and socializing.

This lover of flax (linseed) is resident in fields and hedgerows throughout Europe, western Asia and parts of the Middle East; summer only in parts of its northern range.

LINNET
Linaria cannabina

The delightful linnet, the male resplendent in spring with a bright crimson breast, used to be widely kept in captivity as a cage bird. Despite its attractive appearance, it was the song that enthralled owners. It is a wonderful soliloquy of fast, sweet notes that constantly go off at tangents before being brought back into the thread.

The French have it right. They have an expression, *tête de linotte*, which means to be slightly off your head.

MONTEZUMA OROPENDOLA

Psarocolius montezuma

The oropendolas are a group of tropical American birds famous for building remarkable, pendulous, woven nests, which are often very conspicuously placed high in tall, isolated trees. The Montezuma oropendola is a large Central American species.

These oropendolas form colonies and nests can be concentrated in just one tree. There are usually just a few dozen nests in each, but as many as 172 have been found. The nests take several weeks to weave, and all the work is done by the female. The hanging nests placed at the end of a branch are safe from most nest predators.

The males compete against one another for females by making loud screeching and gurgling noises and hanging upside down by the nests. They try to monopolize the females of neighbouring nests, the more females the better, but just a few dominant males gain access to females. Their mating system has the snappy title of 'female defence polygyny'.

Native to the lowland forests of Central America.

ARARIPE MANAKIN
Antilophia bokermanni

Found only on a single plateau in north-east Brazil.

It's everybody's dream to discover a new species, but imagine what it must have been like to discover this one. That's exactly what happened to Weber de Girao Silva and Artur Galileu Miranda Coelho of the Universidade Federal de Pernambuco as recently as 1996. What an experience it must have been to set eyes upon this ethereal white bird against the sun, its crest lit up like a lamp. The bird, known popularly as *Soldadinho do Araripe* ('The little soldier of Araripe') is found along rivers on a tiny patch of the Chapada do Araripe in north-east Brazil. Its total world breeding range amounts to 10 sq. km (4 sq. miles) and unfortunately it is classified as critically endangered on the International Union for Conservation of Nature's Red List.

GREYLAG GOOSE
Anser anser

Domesticated worldwide. Native breeder in wetland across northern and temperate Eurasia. Asian populations winter well to the south.

On this day, about 2,400 years ago, the course of history was changed by domestic geese. The geese were sacred to the Roman goddess, Juno, and kept in the temple dedicated to her on the Capitoline Hill in ancient Rome, at that time, a prosperous but relatively small city state. During this period, skirmishes took place everywhere, but the most notable European purge was carried out by Celtic Gallic tribes. The Senone Gauls formed part of this group, and it happened that in about 390BCE they launched a violent and entirely unexpected attack on Rome. It was so successful that the Romans fled their outposts and the Gauls sacked most of the city. Only the Capitoline Hill remained intact and the invaders duly besieged it.

During the siege, a Roman messenger climbed up the steep, undefended side of the hill by night to deliver instructions. The Gauls discovered his footprints in the morning and only then realized that there was a way up. They decided to mount an incursion by night and, using their best men, they crept up so quietly that neither the Romans nor their dogs were disturbed from their slumber.

But the geese were and, in their typical way, cackled loudly. A guard called Manlius was awoken and despatched the first invader. Others joined in and the Gauls were repelled. Discouraged and ravaged by illness, they quickly agreed peace terms.

Rome was saved, regrouped and built into the expansionist state that made such a mark on European history over the next 500 years.

L.Lassalle.   Lith Destouches. Paris

EURASIAN MAGPIE
Pica pica

The magpie gets a bad press in folklore. Resident in open woods, parks, gardens in Europe and temperate Asia.

A much-mistrusted ruffian, noisy and bold, the magpie excites emotions as conflicting and contrasting as its black-and-white plumage. Its reputation in folklore as a thief – for example in Rossini's opera *La Gazza Ladra* ('The Thieving Magpie') – is entirely unearned, as it does not collect shiny objects and cache them away. Tales of it stealing wedding rings and other valuables are just that – tales.

The magpie does make itself unpopular with householders, particularly in Britain, for its habit of attacking the nests and nestlings of smaller, beloved birds, such as the blackbird. It often does this in broad daylight, and the raids are unpleasant to watch, but there is no evidence that magpies have any major effect on small-bird populations.

EURASIAN COLLARED DOVE
Streptopelia decaocto

Recognizable by its half collar, this bird often hangs around suburbs and towns from India and Sri Lanka west into Europe; introduced to North America.

One of the world's great invasive species, until the early 20th century the collared dove was found only from Turkey to India and China. Then, in around 1912, it suddenly began to increase its range north and west, colonizing increasingly temperate countries. By the 1950s it had reached Norway and Britain, having expanded at a rate of 44km (27 miles) per annum. By the 1970s, all of Britain and most of Europe was in its grasp. It is still there today, on seemingly every suburban street corner, cooing peacefully.

In the mid-1970s a small group was released in the Bahamas. Some made their way to Florida and another great expansion began, only even faster than the European one. They have now been found in all the lower 48 states and are fast becoming common everywhere.

SOUTHERN ROCKHOPPER PENGUIN
Eudyptes chrysocome

This is the penguin that literally does hop among rocks. On land, it has the appealing habit of jumping two-footed rather than always walking, and regularly falling over. In the water it is a different beast, swimming expertly.

The rockhopper has a curious breeding habit. It always lays two eggs, but the first one is always smaller, hardly ever hatches and, when it does, the chick often dies in the first few days. Why it lays the first egg is a complete mystery.

PALLAS'S SANDGROUSE
Syrrhaptes paradoxus

Sandgrouse are typical of arid and desert areas of the Old World. They are most famous for a unique adaptation to desert life. They nest on the ground and lay 2–3 eggs. When the young hatch they are exposed to the harsh desert sun and require water. The male sandgrouse has evolved specially absorbent feathers on his breast, which soak up water like a sponge. He flies to a water source where he douses himself, flies quickly to the nest, and allows the chicks to drink from his saturated breast.

AFRICAN SACRED IBIS
Threskiornis aethiopicus

Above: Once considered the living incarnation of a god, the ibis still stalks much of sub-Saharan Africa.

Top left: Rockhoppers breed in southern South America and islands plus the subantarctic Indian Ocean.

Bottom left: Found from the Caspian Sea east to Mongolia and China.

In Egypt this date commemorates the revolution of 1952, which marks the establishment of the modern republic. The sacred ibis has been part of Egyptian history for far longer. For 4,500 years this bird has been revered by the inhabitants of the Nile Valley; Ancient Egyptian murals and sculptures are littered with hieroglyphics featuring the sacred ibis. The image of the ibis is a representation of the god Thoth, associated with wisdom and knowledge. During the Twenty-sixth Dynasty (664–525BCE), the sacred ibis became the subject of a widespread cult, in which the birds were mummified and placed in catacombs as religious offerings to bring good fortune. The birds themselves were usually bred in captivity to keep up with supply, which was not easy. At one site in Egypt, Tuna-el-Gebel, 270km (168 miles) south of Cairo, there are more than 4 million embalmed birds, with 1.75 million at Saqqara, near the ancient city of Hermopolis. The cult continued right into the Roman era, surviving until at least 390CE.

SCISSOR-TAILED FLYCATCHER
Tyrannus forficatus

The state bird of Oklahoma since 1951, featured here on a quarter. The bird breeds in open country of south central USA and winters in Central America.

More an apparition than a bird, this stunner is found in the southern United States, migrating to Central America in the winter. It is common on overhead wires and other raised perches in open country, where it watches the ground below or the immediate airspace for large insects, which it catches in a quick sally to the ground or a dashing pursuit-flight. One of its favourite food items is grasshoppers.

Both males and females are adorned with remarkable, elongated tail-streamers. However, the male's tail is significantly longer and varies between individuals. Not surprisingly, females prefer the males with the longest tails, an easily appreciated demonstration of physical fitness.

Lyrebirds are great mimics and learn more 'songs' as they get older. About now they can be found singing in rainforests of south-eastern Australia.

SUPERB LYREBIRD
Menura novaehollandiae

An Australian icon, the superb lyrebird lives in the forests of the south-east. It is a large songbird, which looks and acts like a small pheasant, using its feet to scratch at the leaf litter to find food. Although sometimes shy, it can also be seen around parking lots and picnic areas in national parks. It often sings lustily in the middle of winter.

This bird's fame rests with its spectacular song-display, in which the opulent lyre-tailed plumes are raised over the bird's back to create a canopy, and from its extraordinary ability to mimic sounds. About 70 per cent of the fast and complex song, which sounds like a recording of a forest dawn chorus, is mimicry of the local birds, usually about 20 imitated species per individual lyrebird. What appeals to many people, though, are the non-avian impressions. These can include koalas, frogs, pigs, whistling humans and, occasionally, mechanical sounds such as starting cars, photographer's motor-drives, saws, car alarms and, apparently, the crackling of flames in a fire. These imitations are copied down the generations, so the sound of some bird species that have been lost in the habitat could be retained for many years by the songs of a lyrebird.

COMMON WOOD PIGEON
Columba palumbus

Abundant in woods and farmland of Western Europe east to southern Asia; migrant in the east and north of its range.

The throaty, somewhat saucy croon of the wood pigeon could perhaps be the most familiar bird song in Western Europe. While other species shout for short bursts in spring, the wood pigeon carries on vocalizing throughout the summer into early autumn. Go to a British wood in July or August and the reassuring sound will envelop you, soothe you and cool you.

The birds themselves are handsome, too, and for much of the year they engage in a lively flight display, launching themselves from an elevated perch to fly upwards at a sharp angle, sometimes with a wing clap or two. Then, as if they have been shot, they become rigid, holding their wings out and gliding down until they come to rest 50m (160ft) or more away in a straight line from where they started.

Despite their high jinks, few people appreciate wood pigeons, and many people loathe them. They raid agricultural crops and do a great deal of damage. The comforting song is not quite enough.

PHAINOPEPLA
Phainopepla nitens

Found in desert and arid woods of south-west North America and northern Mexico, this flycatcher is unique for its breeding pattern.

Right now you are probably thinking, 'What a terrible name for a bird.' However, when you learn that *phainopepla* is Greek for 'shining robe', a reference to the male's glossy black plumage, it doesn't sound so bad.

The phainopepla is the split personality of North American birds, exhibiting profoundly different behaviour at different times of year. From February to April it breeds in the Sonoran Desert of Arizona and California, feeding on mistletoe berries. Pairs defend discrete territories from all-comers, often in a highly aggressive manner. From May onwards it breeds instead in oak and sycamore woodland, feeding on a range of berries and, bizarrely, then resorts to colonial breeding, with pairs co-operating in defending the trees in which they are nesting from predators, and living peacefully in close proximity.

Breeding twice in the same year, in different habitats and in a completely different social structure, is entirely unique.

RED-WHISKERED BULBUL
Pycnonotus jocosus

These birds ar found in the forest and gardens of southern Asia, from India east to China. They are easily tamed and can be taught to sit on a hand.

The scientific name *jocosus* means 'merry', and there's no doubting that the irrepressible red-whiskered bulbul lives up to that epithet. This is a common bird in southern Asia, where it mixes with people in cities, gardens and open areas near cultivation. Here, the bird's simple, relatively melodious but markedly cheery song, is part of the soundscape familiar to millions of people.

Red-whiskered bulbuls are birds with simple lifestyles, non-migratory, without awkward feeding requirements or curious breeding arrangements. As a result it has often thrived when introduced to new places, such as Hawaii, Australia (where it is abundant in Sydney), Mauritius, Florida and California.

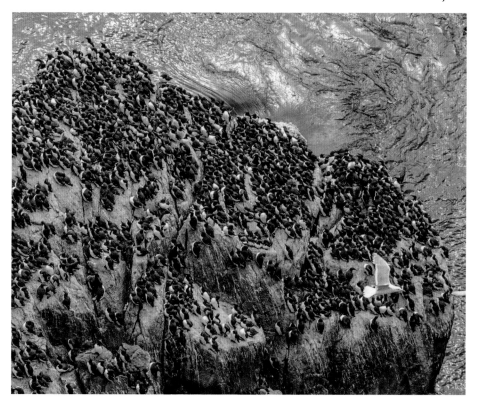

GUILLEMOT (COMMON MURRE)
Uria aalge

From temperate to Arctic rocky shores and cliffs of the North Atlantic and North Pacific, guillemots nest in noisy colonies.

The guillemot looks like a flying penguin, and it inhabits sea cliffs in the northern hemisphere. It doesn't build a nest, but often lays its single egg on a narrow edge at terrifying heights above the sea, cheek by jowl with its near neighbours.

After three weeks of being fed by both adults, the chick will have grown enough to leave its precipitous perch. Now the role of the father becomes vital. It calls incessantly to its chick and the chick calls back. Sometimes the father settles on the water below and calls, or it stands next to the chick as the latter contemplates jumping. With poorly developed wings, lacking the main flight feathers, it is a risky prospect.

Eventually, as evening falls (or as the sky reaches its darkest point) the chick jumps. It may fall 300m (1,000ft) before landing in the sea. There it meets its father and the two swim off. It is thought that adult and progeny remain together for a month or more far offshore.

213

NORTHERN FLICKER
Colaptes auratus

To many people, woodpeckers are birds of the trees, and the last place you might expect to find one is on the ground. However, the northern flicker is among a significant number of woodpeckers that are most at home on the deck, and these are usually ant specialists. This species probably eats more ants than any other North American bird. It will spend hours at a nest, picking off the insects one by one, lapping them up with its sticky tongue, which extends 4cm (1½in) beyond the bill tip. It usually avoids the more aggressive species, though, which is a shame for those who are plagued by them.

Although a terrestrial bird, the northern flicker still makes a hole in a tree for its nest like other woodpeckers. A common bird, it is a so-called 'keystone' species, providing habitat for other birds and animals with its carpentry expertise.

Licking up ants across North America and into Central America; summer visitor to most of Canada.

EURASIAN HOBBY
Falco subbuteo

Fast and furious, the hobby's summer hobby is catching dragonflies. Breeding now across much of temperate Eurasia in open country with trees, it winters in sub-Saharan Africa and parts of India.

It's high summer in Europe, and the heat has turbo-charged the insects, none more so than the dragonflies. Large, fast and with keen vision, these aerial dashers revel in the sun on their backs, and they sail the four winds on four wings, making them extraordinarily agile and unpredictable. Few predators can catch them.

However, one that most certainly can is the hobby, an equally dashing bird of prey, with scimitar wings and a similar line in fast manoeuvring. Dragonflies are its preferred diet at this time of the year, and several individuals may gather together at favoured sites, such as large areas of wetland or heathland. Here, with a combination of sheer speed and a long reach with their talons, hobbies can snatch the fastest dragonflies out of the sky and transfer them to their bills in mid-air.

The hobby is exclusively an aerial predator. Its exceptional abilities mean that it can also catch swallows, and even swifts.

BLACK-THROATED GREEN WARBLER
Setophaga virens

Still singing in coniferous forests in north-eastern North America and the Appalachians; winters on the Gulf Coast, Caribbean and down to northern South America.

In the conifer woods of north-eastern North America the warmth has sucked the life out of the atmosphere, which resembles something like the morning after a wild party. In many ways it is, with the breeding frenzy over and birds going around quietly, as if they are suffering from hangovers. The voices of spring have faded away.

Except for one. Even on these quiet days, the song of the black-throated green warbler can be heard: 'Trees, trees, murmuring trees' it goes, plaintive in the silence. It is often a broken phrase these days, '... murmuring trees', but it's always there. It comes from America's evergreen warbler – living in evergreens, singing to the last and never losing its fresh, spring-green plumage, even when it becomes a so-called 'confusing fall warbler' when the plumage changes from breeding to non-breeding.

PIED AVOCET
Recurvirostra avosetta

The avocet's beak is perfectly designed for its job, foraging across saline wetlands over much of the Old World, but not Australasia.

Many of the world's birds have bills that bend downwards, known as decurved. However, comparatively few have bills that curve upwards, recurved. No bird models its recurved bill as elegantly and prominently as the pied avocet (and its three related species).

The shape of the bill is thought to come about from the avocet's most prominent feeding action, scything. Avocets feed mainly in saline water, catching shrimps and small fish. Scything is the process of swishing their slightly opened bill from side to side in the shallows or the mud, hoping to hit something solid. Since avocets need to wade to make this work, they lean down into the water, and the bill shape has simply evolved to ensure that it is almost horizontal while it is being scythed, allowing a greater touch-sensitive surface area to be exposed to the water. A bent bill also allows the bill to open to the same width throughout its length – a straight bill would be wider at the tip.

WOODPECKER FINCH
Camarhynchus pallidus

Above: This bird of the Galapagos Islands regularly goes spear hunting.

Top right: Found in grasslands across sub-Saharan West Africa, central Africa and extreme east of southern Africa.

Bottom right: A hunter of the Arctic and temperate coasts of the North Atlantic.

The woodpecker finch is a member of the group known as Darwin's finches, native to the Galapagos, where it is found on most of the islands and at all altitudes. While the other finches are known for having different-shaped bills, and for their remarkable niche separation, the woodpecker finch is known for something quite unrelated. It is a tool-user, the only one of its group to be so, and one of the very few songbirds.

It uses tools during its explorations for insects, particularly grubs. It often uses a cactus spine or a typical leaf and will use it to gouge at grubs in holes. It might fashion the tool by, for example, breaking it in two, and favoured spines are often reused. Interestingly, the degree of tool use varies between islands.

The bill of the woodpecker finch is slightly longer than that of many other Darwin's finches, and this finch has a broader diet than many.

YELLOW-THROATED LONGCLAW
Macronyx croceus

Longclaws are ground birds found in sub-Saharan Africa. They are perhaps most famous for their remarkable similarity to the much better-known, but completely unrelated meadowlarks of North America (see page 167).

The similarity doesn't just cover their physical appearance. Both longclaws and meadowlarks are found in grassland, and have similar styles of flight, nesting behaviour and general habits. It is a stunning example of convergent evolution.

GREAT BLACK-BACKED GULL
Larus marinus

Not everyone appreciates gulls, so if you are the largest and meanest gull species in the neighbourhood, the chances are that you are not going to be popular. The great black-back is one of the most predatory of gulls. It regularly attacks and eats seabirds of various kinds, such as the beloved puffin; individuals scour seabird colonies for careless parents and vulnerable chicks. It has even been seen munching contentedly on a human corpse!

GREAT KISKADEE
Pitangus sulphuratus

This American flycatcher will also eat fruit – and peanut butter sandwiches. It is abundant in open habitats throughout South America and Central America, north to Texas.

One of the most common birds in all the warm regions of the Americas, the great kiskadee is a bird of open country and has adapted well to human environments. It is large, brightly coloured and noisy, with its loud three-note call giving rise to its English common name, as well as the French *Qu'est-ce qu'il dit?* and the Portuguese *Bien-te-veo*.

A member of a family of flycatchers, the great kiskadee uses the signature method of waiting on an elevated perch and then flying out to grab flying insects. But this large flycatcher has adapted this basic foraging method to expand its diet vastly. It has been known to eat tadpoles (especially of bullfrogs), rodents, snails, small snakes, lizards and even fish. Sometimes it even apes a kingfisher by hovering over the water and plunging down. Maybe the French name should be *Qu'est-ce qu'il mange?*

LAMMERGEIER
Gypaetus barbatus

A bone-crunching vulture that keeps to the mountains of Europe, Asia and parts of East Africa.

Birds around the world can survive on some strange diets, but few are quite so niche as the magnificent lammergeier, a huge and imperious vulture of Eurasia and Africa. It eats bones, which comprise 85 per cent of its diet.

Despite its large size, the lammergeier does not, therefore, need to compete at traditional vulture scrums. Instead it can wait until the other birds have had their fill and gorge itself on all the barely digestible parts of the carcass, the skeleton, skin and other titbits. Its stomach contains unusually high levels of acid.

Bones can be awkward to handle, and sometimes need to be broken before they can be swallowed, so the lammergeier will soar up into the sky and drop larger bones so that they are smashed on the rocks below. This also releases the tasty marrow. Unfortunately, lammergeiers will also do this to tortoises, which suffer the same fate.

WHITE-TAILED TROPICBIRD
Phaethon lepturus

A seabird of the tropics, breeding on islands in the Indian, Atlantic and west Pacific Oceans; otherwise wanders.

It is hard to imagine a lovelier sea bird to admire as you sail the warm waters of the tropics. Tropicbirds are supremely aerial sea birds that wander the world's oceans, often at vast distances from land. To catch food, they plunge-dive from a height that may reach over 50m (160ft), frequently spiralling as they plummet downwards. Their main food is fish – especially flying fish – and squid. Tropicbirds have fully waterproof plumage and will rest on the surface of the sea.

Their long tail-plumes wear out quickly and, unlike the rest of the tail, are continually replaced.

SCREAMING PIHA
Lipaugus vociferans

Amazonian lowland forests of northern and central South America ring out with the song of this screecher.

If you are lucky enough to visit the lowland rainforest of the Amazon, the loud call of the piha is one of the dominant sounds you will hear – a three-syllable 'Qui-qui-yo', with the last syllable pitched lower. It goes on all day.

The sound may travel 400m (1,300ft) through the rainforest, and it has been measured at a 1m (3¼ft) range as 115.5 decibels, registering somewhere between 'discomfort' and 'pain.'

New Caledonian Crow
Corvus moneduloides

These clever crows from the forests of New Caledonia fashion their own tools.

It is truly extraordinary that a crow from a somewhat obscure island off the north-east coast of Australia should rank as one of the world's most intelligent birds – indeed, all living organisms. It is foremost among all birds in its use of tools, a rare trait.

In their native land, these birds are famous for fashioning tools from leaves. Taking a pandanus leaf, they use their bill to form it into a spear-like shape, which they insert into the burrow of their favourite food – large, juicy grubs. The grubs grab the end of the spear in defence and are rapidly pulled out. Using the tool is the only way to reach this highly nutritious meal.

The crows also make other tools of different patterns, each for a different purpose. Why this particular species should have evolved such skills is a mystery.

AMERICAN WHITE PELICAN
Pelecanus erythrorhynchos

Of all American birds, this one's wingspan is second only to the Californian condor. They summer and breed now on lakes, marshes and rivers in midwest North America; winters in California and Gulf Coast region, into Central America.

On this day in 2019 a large hailstorm swept across the Big Lake Wildlife Management Area in Montana, USA. Hailstorms are nothing new, of course, but this one was so powerful that it broke the windows and even the roofs of nearby cars and houses.

Its effect on the local water birds, among them pelicans and cormorants, was devastating. In just a few minutes there were more than 11,000 casualties, either killed or badly injured. Some of the hailstones were as large as baseballs.

So spare a thought for wild birds caught up in extreme weather events. For us, a hailstorm is a curiosity; for them it can mean fractured skulls, broken wings and death.

DODO
Raphus cucullatus

The dodo is perhaps the most famous extinct bird in the world. This bizarre icon epitomizes the reality of the loss of nature.

It is a frustrating icon, undoubtedly extraordinary yet never grasped in an adequate scientific net. We don't know exactly when it was discovered, although the first written account was in 1599; we don't even know when it became extinct, the likelihood being between 1662 and 1693. And we don't know why it became extinct. Amazingly, it is almost certain that a live dodo was exhibited in London in 1638 and in India around the same time, but nothing was recorded about it then and virtually nothing was observed in the wild. It almost certainly ate fruit, but the rest of its lifestyle is a mystery. Even its appearance is uncertain, from its size to its colour. There are only a couple of reliable contemporary illustrations and there are no complete specimens. Most remains are sub-fossil. We know considerably more about *Tyrannosaurus rex*, which became extinct 65 million years ago, that we do about a bird that has been lost for just over 300 years.

GUANAY CORMORANT
Leucocarbo bougainvillii

Guanay
cormorants and
Peruvian pelicans
on cliffs and
islands along the
Pacific coasts of
South America.
They are both
suppliers of
finest guano, the
ideal fertilizer.

This is one of three species of 'guano birds' found off the coast of Peru and celebrated above all else for their production of excrement. This, the Peruvian booby and the Peruvian pelican nest in enormous numbers on islands off this curious coastline, where the cold-water Humboldt Current brings bounteous nutrients from the sea bed and drives a marine ecosystem of astounding productivity, yet it lies adjacent to the Atacama, the driest desert in the world, which is often shrouded in fog. The complete lack of rain ensures that the guano built up by generations of breeding sea birds is ineffably rich in nutrients, such as phosphates and nitrates. The Inca knew about this richness, and carefully and sustainably protected the sea bird islands. But latterly, for a short while in the mid-1800s, harvesting the vast piles of guano, some up to 50m (165ft) thick, became an important industry, and in 30 years about 20 million tonnes were exported. Populations of the guano birds inevitably crashed. Since then, however, following protection, the species have recovered their numbers.

ELEONORA'S FALCON
Falco eleonorae

Chicks now being fed on offshore islands in the Mediterranean region and off the coast of North Africa; migrates to winter in Madagascar.

It's mid-August, and most birds in the northern temperate regions of the world have finished breeding. However, at a few sites around the Mediterranean, there is a bird whose eggs are just beginning to hatch, the remarkable Eleonora's falcon.

The reason for this is simple: the journeys of migratory northern birds to their wintering grounds is in full swing. And what do Eleonora's falcons bring to feed their young in the nest? Small migratory birds. They take advantage of the streams of migrants passing by, a constant source of food on which to nourish their own young.

As every birder knows, some days are better for migrating than others – a following air stream encourages the travellers to fly, whereas bad weather causes migration to halt. So the Eleonora's falcons catch far more that they or their chicks need on good days, and store it away to cover for bad days.

As a macabre twist, it seems that some Eleonora's falcons store their caches live. Small warblers have been found apparently imprisoned in rock crevices, unable to get out and evidently put there by the predators.

CLARK'S NUTCRACKER
Nucifraga columbiana

Collecting seeds now, this bird has an interdependent relationship with its main food source, the whitebark pine, found in high mountain conifer forests of western North America.

This remarkable bird of the mountains of the North American west relies on one type of food above all others – the seeds of conifers. It eats them from the trees when available, but from mid-summer onwards takes great steps to cache them away in a multitude of hiding places, usually on the ground in leaf litter. In this way, if harsh conditions prevail in the winter, it has a ready store of food available. In a single year, a Clark's nutcracker has been known to store away 100,000 seeds.

When collecting seeds for its larders, it makes use of a remarkable anatomical quirk, almost entirely unique, a pouch under its palate. This can expand greatly, so that nutcrackers carrying seeds in their pouch exhibit a great bulge at the throat when they are flying. A single bird can carry 150 seeds of the whitebark pine at one time. To make this system work, the Clark's nutcracker also needs extraordinary powers of memory – could you find 100,000 items you had hidden away, or even 1,000 for that matter? And the bird must also rely on its spatial awareness, even to follow up what it has remembered. It is, by any measure, an impressive feat.

This rare, highly protected bird deserves its place on a stamp. Introduced to a few offshore islands off South Island, New Zealand, its rare speckled feathers provide perfect camouflage.

KAKAPO
Strigops habroptila

The kakapo of New Zealand is an extraordinary bird. It is the world's only living flightless parrot and the only truly nocturnal member of that family. It is the only flightless bird to have a method of breeding known as a lek, in which males compete alongside each other for females, the latter choosing just one for copulation, with no further help in feeding or raising the young. It is also one of the world's longest-lived birds, with an average lifespan of 60 years, and is one of the world's most completely vegetarian bird species. And it's a miracle that it is still with us.

Before people arrived in New Zealand, the kakapo was widespread. The indigenous peoples began its decline by killing kakapo for meat and feather ornaments and cutting down forests, and this rate accelerated with the arrival of Europeans, who added insult to injury by introducing animals and plants that degraded the habitat, and either ate the kakapo or their eggs and young. As long ago as 1891, the New Zealand government recognized that the kakapo were declining and moved a population to Resolution Island. However, predatory stoats arrived and wiped them out. By the 1970s the kakapo was thought to be on the verge of extinction, with the group in Fiordland consisting only of males. Fortunately, in 1977 a population was discovered on Stewart Island, which did include females, and this population has formed the nucleus of an astonishing recovery. Over the years, birds have been translocated to predator-free offshore islands and much effort and study has gone into working out how they can thrive. Females are given supplementary food in the breeding season, while in the early days, traps were set near nests to prevent predation by rats. Little by little, breeding rates increased, and the population has inched upwards.

These days, the kakapo population is about 150 birds, each and every one a marvel of conservation.

TURKEY VULTURE
Cathartes aura

Very common
over much of
the Americas, in
many habitats.
Summer visitor
to northern and
western range in
North America.

There are many vultures around the world, not all closely related, but all are scavengers – essentially relying on eating dead animals. Remarkably, the turkey vulture of the Americas is the only one that can smell dead meat; the rest rely solely on their exceptional eyesight.

A really good sense of smell is rare in birds, so the turkey vulture should have a competitive advantage. However, over most of its range it has a rival, the stockier and much more aggressive black vulture, a bird that will sometimes follow turkey vultures around. Fortunately for the turkey vulture, however, its sense of smell allows it to find small, recently dead animals rather than large, putrid carcasses. This means that the turkey vulture can usually quickly find and eat what it needs before being interrupted.

STRIATED HERON
Butorides striata

Lure fishers of the bird world. Found in many warm parts of the world, including Central and South America, Australasia, Africa and southern Asia.

Herons have something of a primitive look, so it might come as a considerable surprise to learn that they can be highly intelligent. The geniuses of the family are the striated heron of the Old World and its close relative, the green heron of the Americas, and their party trick is to use bait to catch fish.

Smaller than the average heron, at around 44cm (17in), these birds use lures of various kinds to attract curious fish, including broken twigs, feathers, bread and even human artefacts such as plastic foam. Remarkably, they also use live bait like mayflies and other invertebrates, which unsurprisingly is more successful. One bird was even seen to dig up earthworms from the shore and throw them on to the water's surface. Now that is clever!

SCARLET MACAW
Ara macao

A pair of scarlet macaws in their natural habitat – lowland tropical forests of Central and South America, especially Amazonia.

There are few more magnificent sights than macaws flying over their rainforest home. Huge, with long, trailing tails, they fly over the treetops with slow, deep wing beats, pairs often co-ordinating their flight in perfect harmony. As they go, they give their magnificent harsh, screeching calls, among the loudest made by any birds, which echo over the canopy. In the morning sun, the scarlet macaw glows in a riot of crimson, yellow and electric blue.

This is a classic Amazonian bird, which also ranges into Central America. For centuries macaws have been worshipped by Amerindians and their feathers are regularly a major feature of headdresses. The birds also make good pets, from Amazonian villages to cities in the west, where their talking ability and tendency to be affectionate endears them to owners. Their home, though, is the pristine forest canopy.

DUSKY GROUSE
Dendragapus obscurus

A male dusky grouse. For this high-altitude bird of western North America, migration to conifer forest is just a walk in the park.

This is the time of year that many a bird breeding at northern latitudes will wake up, sniff the air, proverbially sigh and put its rucksack on its back. It is the beginning of the great annual migration to warmer climates.

The dusky grouse is one such migrant. However, it has a most unusual distinction – that of having the shortest migration in the world. It doesn't move latitudes to avoid bad weather, but instead shifts altitudes, and between habitats.

One dusky grouse in Oregon was recorded moving only 400m (1,300ft) from breeding grounds to wintering grounds. Others, though, may travel up to 50km (31 miles), a distance that some individuals can walk.

And then, at the end of the day, they can put their feet up a few hundred metres downhill and feel satisfied at a job well done!

GREY CROWNED CRANE
Balearica regulorum

Cranes are tall, graceful birds with a regal manner, walking in stately fashion over grassland and marsh, and flying with deep, slow wing beats. The grey crowned crane, an East African species that is the national bird of Uganda (and features on its flag), is further endowed with a splendid head-dress of yellowish plumes.

One of the joys of cranes is their spontaneous displaying, which includes bowing, stretching and leaping into the air with their wings half open. Cranes mate for life, and pairs may dance at any time of year. The display is infectious, and when birds are in a large flock, many pairs at once may launch into this delightful routine, turning a field into a crane ballroom.

Above: A courtly pair of cranes. Found in grassland and wetlands of east and southern Africa.

Top right: A bird of South and Central America and southern half of North America.

Bottom right: A desert bird of southern USA and Mexico.

SNOWY EGRET
Egretta thula

The snowy egret is a resourceful hunter and uses no less than 21 different methods for catching fish and crustaceans in the water. These are:

1. standing; 2. bill vibrating; 3. head swaying; 4. pecking; 5. walking slowly; 6. walking quickly; 7. running; 8. hopping; 9. leapfrog feeding; 10. wing flicking; 11. open wing feeding; 12. underwing feeding; 13. foot stirring; 14. foot raking; 15. foot probing; 16. foot paddling; 17. hovering; 18. hover stirring; 19. dipping; 20. disturb and chase; 21. foot-dragging.

CACTUS WREN
Campylorhynchus brunneicapillus

A classic desert bird, the North American cactus wren is found in a range of dry habitats. It often builds its domed nest inside a thorny bush or cactus, such as the candelabra-shaped giant saguaro.

An individual cactus wren can live its whole life without ever drinking. It acquires all its fluids from its diet of fruit, insects and other invertebrates.

RESPLENDENT QUETZAL
Pharomachrus mocinno

Quetzalcoatl was an Aztec god of the air, and the iridescent green feathers of the resplendent quetzal were linked to him. The bird is found in montane forests of Central America, from southern Mexico to Panama.

With its sparkling, iridescent green plumage, brilliant crimson belly and extraordinary long, shimmering tail feathers, the male resplendent quetzal has always held people in its thrall. In Central America, where it lives, it was worshipped by the Mayans and the Aztecs. Quetzalcoatl was the god of all good things, and rulers required the feathers of the quetzal for headdresses. Even today, the quetzal adorns the flag of Guatemala, one of the countries where it occurs, and gives its name to the official currency of the country.

Not bad for a bird that spends much of its day sitting still or gobbling fruit. Avocados are a favourite.

BROWN PELICAN
Pelecanus occidentalis

These anchovy eaters prefer the warmer coasts of North, Central and northern South America.

If you can tear your eyes away from the beautiful people on the beaches of California and Florida, you might well spot another common resident of this habitat – the brown pelican. Along with the Peruvian pelican (*P. thagus*), this is the only marine member of the pelican family. You can often see 'squadrons' of these huge birds flying in formation just above the wave tops or high in the air. Pelicans are famous for their capacious bills, carrying up to 9–14 litres (2–3 gallons) of water, which they use as fishing nets, scooping up and then draining the water to leave moderate-sized fish *in situ*. The brown pelican has a different take on the usual method of fishing employed by fellow pelicans: it plunge dives into the water from a height of up to 20m (66ft) above the surface and scoops up water during its full-body immersion. Although this means that it doesn't compete with other species, unfortunately cunning gulls will sometimes nip in and steal the catch – another kind of scoop.

EURASIAN TREE SPARROW
Passer montanus

These sparrows are happy in the rural and urban habitats of Europe and Asia, also Indonesia.

In Europe, this is the 'other' sparrow, the smaller, more delicately and precisely plumaged relative of the ubiquitous house sparrow. In many ways it is the 'acceptable' countryside sparrow, less grimy and messy, less dependent on people and found in more pleasant environments. In the UK, it has declined sharply for years and is of major conservation concern.

And yet, head eastwards and, quite suddenly, it is the tree sparrow that is everywhere – in China, southern Asia and Japan. Here, in the absence of the dominant house sparrow, the tree sparrow occupies the urban niche and is a bird of streets, gardens and farmland. The switch is extraordinary.

COMMON OSTRICH
Struthio camelus

On Africa's plains and deserts where the ostrich breeds, its egg is a big prize for predators such as hyaenas, jackals and vultures. It has a volume 24 times the average chicken egg, weighs 1.3–1.9kg (3–4lb) and measures about 14–18cm (5½–7in) long; that's a lot of tasty biomass. And in a typical ostrich nest, incubated by both male and female, there are 20 such eggs.

Although both adults protect the eggs physically, they also have a much more cunning way to keep them safe. Each male and its primary mate, the so-called major hen, allow a succession of other females, called minor hens, to lay their own eggs in the same nest. The clever part is that they arrange the nest so that the eggs of the major hen are on the inside, and the eggs of the minor hens are on the outside. A predator raiding the nest is more likely to make off with an easily reached peripheral egg.

The minor hens' eggs, therefore, act as a buffer for the precious eggs of the major hen. The occasional minor hen's egg survives, too, which is why they bother to use the major hen's nest.

The largest bird eggs in the world belong to the ostrich, which resides all year round in arid scrub and plains of Sub-Saharan Africa.

WHITE-RUMPED SHAMA
Kittacincla malabarica

A male of the species – the female in greyish-brown. Found in forest edge and gardens in warmer parts of Asia and Indonesia.

The nightingale of the east, and with similar retiring habits, the white-rumped shama is one of the world's great songbirds. Its gorgeous, deep, rich and powerful notes are interspersed with much mimicry of other birds. In parts of south Asia it is a common cage bird, and dealers compete over the individuals with the richest voices and the longest tails.

A notable claim to fame is that the white-rumped shama features in the earliest bird-sound recording ever made. It is a phonograph recording on wax cylinders, made by the German Ludwig Koch in 1889, when he was only eight years old. The bird was a family pet.

Bar-tailed Godwit
Limosa lapponica

This long-distance flier breeds in the high Arctic tundra of Eurasia and Alaska; winters on coasts in Australasia, Eurasia and Africa.

On this day in 2007, a bar-tailed godwit called E7 left Kuskokwim Shoals, Alaska, USA, and set off on her flight south, just as millions of birds breeding in northern latitudes do as autumn bites. The only difference was that this bird was embarking on a journey that would astonish scientists and change the way we think about bird migration.

Amazingly satellite-tagged E7 flew for eight consecutive days and nights. It was impossible to make landfall, because she flew across the open expanse of the Pacific Ocean. Only when reaching Miranda, on the north coast of New Zealand on 7 September, did E7 finally touch down. This remains the longest flight of any land bird ever recorded, at nearly 11,700km (7,264 miles).

COMMON RAVEN
Corvus corax

A raven stands guard at the Tower of London, UK. Found widely in Europe, Asia and North America.

The world's largest songbird, the raven is as big as a medium-sized raptor. Its slow, imperious wing beats, deep, croaking voice and entirely black plumage have long conferred on it a sinister air, and its relationship with people has not always been comfortable. In past times, the raven would have been a constant presence at any gallows, and would have attended the aftermath of battles, attracted by the ready supply of corpses on which to scavenge. No wonder it has long held an association with death, and often a certain feared respect.

The irony is that, belying its sombre image, the raven is one of the world's most intelligent species of birds. It commonly indulges in acts of playfulness, a sudden, upside-down roll when flying in a straight line or acrobatic in-flight manoeuvres. Young birds sometimes hang upside-down, like bats. In addition, pairs of ravens, which usually remain together for life, will often call to each other in a kind of pet language all of their own.

EDIBLE-NEST SWIFTLET
Aerodramus fuciphagus

This nest is a delicacy – if you like that sort of thing. You can find one in caves in south-east Asia and the Indonesian archipelago.

One day, hundreds or maybe thousands of years ago, somebody came up with the idea of eating the saliva of a bird. It is an extraordinary thought, but this is the main ingredient of genuine bird's-nest soup, a delicacy that has long been enjoyed in many parts of Asia. So prized are the nests that, until recently, people would risk their lives using bamboo ladders to reach the swiftlets' nests, which the birds place in the roofs and high walls of huge, dark caves (and the birds use echolocation to get around). The caves are desperately unhygienic – the floors covered with mounds of foul-smelling bird excreta – there are hordes of unattractive invertebrates with too many legs, the air is full of spores harmful to the lungs and the scaffolds are rickety. All this in the name of selling spit.

PASSENGER PIGEON

Ectopistes migratorius

On 1 September 1914, just before 1pm, the world lost some its environmental innocence. On that day the last surviving passenger pigeon died at the Cincinnati Zoo & Botanical Gardens, Ohio, USA. Extinctions had happened before, but this was different; just 100 years previously the passenger pigeon had probably been the most prolific bird species on Earth. Overhunting in the 19th century killed it and the species was lost forever.

2ᴺᴰ SEPTEMBER

GRAY CATBIRD

Dumetella carolinensis

Named for its call, a kind of mewing, the catbird is a common North American species. It also has a remarkably complex song, with hundreds of syllables all combined into a rambling monologue. The female catbird lays blue-green eggs. It happens that the best and most healthy females lay the brightest clutches. The brilliant colour stimulates the male to put in more effort feeding the young than he otherwise would, since the progeny from these eggs will also be of high quality.

Above: Not a dinosaur, but still rare and found in dense swamps of east-central Africa.

Top left: Once in deciduous forests of eastern North America. Extinct.

Bottom left: The catbird nests in the rush and undergrowth of east and central North America; migrates south to Central America and Caribbean.

SHOEBILL

Balaeniceps rex

You'd think that only a mother could love the bizarre shoebill, but it turns out that birders love them, too. They are unique, strange, very rare and occur only in the richest African swamps.

Neither a stork, nor a heron, the shoebill is not closely related to anything. The outsize bill is used for grabbing fish from shallow water enmeshed with a tangle of vegetation. The bird lunges forwards from a standing position, sometimes falling in, and isolates the food with its bill before extracting itself. The bill is also good for holding water, sometimes giving the chicks in the nest a shower.

Lungfish and other heavies are a favourite, but the shoebill has also been known to take young crocodiles. The reptiles return the 'favour', eating young shoebills, but this giant wading bird has few other predators.

SPECKLED MOUSEBIRD
Colius striatus

Mousebirds are oddities. Occurring only in sub-Saharan Africa, they have soft, greyish plumage and peculiar feet, which allow them a trapeze artist's expertise in navigating their way through thick vegetation. The way they scurry around makes you wonder whether, at some point in the distant past, some stray rodent DNA found its way in, hence the name. They often cling on to a perch with their feet, as if they are trying to peer over a wall.

Common in gardens and bushland, mousebirds are extreme vegetarians. They can eat every berry that they find, no matter how noxious, even those that would kill a human within hours. When they are not eating they can be found resting in semi-torpor, their body temperature lowered. Living in groups, they are always huddled together, like hikers trapped in a mountain by a storm.

The mousebirds have no living relatives. Their dead relatives, though, are legion and mousebirds were once fixtures of both the Eurasian and North American avifauna.

A huddle of mousebirds. They are common in thick bush and gardens in much of sub-Saharan Africa.

COMMON RINGED PLOVER
Charadrius hiaticula

Small and dumpy for a wading bird, the plover is surprisingly successful. Breeds on coasts and shingle of Western Europe, Greenland and northern Eurasia; winters Europe, Near East and Africa.

Look at the ringed plover in a picture like this and it is striking, perhaps even conspicuous. In real life, however, especially at a distance, the bold black collar and patches around the eyes break up the bird's outline and distract the observer, making it almost impossible to see. This is known as 'disruptive camouflage'.

GREATER HONEYGUIDE
Indicator indicator

A bird of woodland and savanna in much of sub-Saharan Africa.

One of the most remarkable relationships between birds and humans takes place in tropical Africa, in the bush country. It takes place between Africans living off the land and the greater honeyguide. No one knows when the symbiosis began, but it is likely to be very ancient.

The greater honeyguide feeds mainly on invertebrates but also has a favourite snack: beeswax. The bird can raid bees' nests and take its own wax, but over the centuries honeyguides have somehow learned that humans are excellent at breaking into bee colonies. Humans have proved to be so useful that honeyguides have also learned to summon them and lead them to hives, hoping that they will open up the colonies and expose the wax.

Thus, when a honeyguide is aware of the presence of a bee colony, it finds some people and makes a loud call, one usually associated with aggression, hoping that the humans will respond. If they do, the honeyguide will make conspicuous flying movements in the direction of the food supply, and flash its white outer tail feather while calling continuously. When it reaches the bees' nest, it falls silent. If it has found a group of brave and knowledgeable African hunters, it will reap the rewards. The men are somehow able to cope with the pain and potential danger of being repeatedly stung. First they light a smoky fire to stupefy the bees, and then they break open the nest with a machete. The hunters take the honey, while the bird gets pieces of comb, wax and bee larvae. Both are satisfied, and the symbiosis is complete.

BOBOLINK
Dolichonyx oryzivorus

The much-loved bobolink has to be the best-dressed bird in North America, with the male's sharp-suited, tuxedo-like plumage and immaculate demeanour. On the hay-meadows and damp fields of the east, males are even more eye-catching as they perform helicopter-like song-flights over the weed tops. The song is fun, if not especially tuneful, with much bubbling and gurgling, which just about accounts for this bird's unusual name.

Each fall, bobolinks embark on a remarkable long migration that may take them 10,000km (6,200 miles) southwards. They make an extended stop of several weeks in Venezuela or Colombia, then stay over in Bolivia and finally arrive on the plains of central South America, embracing Brazil, Paraguay and Argentina, up to four months later.

A male (top) and female bobolink. These long-haul fliers breed in old fields and meadows over much of north temperate North America; they migrate to grasslands of central South America.

SWORD-BILLED HUMMINGBIRD
Ensifera ensifera

The extraordinary sword-billed hummingbird is the only bird in the world whose bill is longer than the rest of its body and so is its tongue. It is the sort of bird whose existence you might doubt if it were not for the many photographs taken across its range in the humid montane forest of the Andes. When perching, it has to hold its bill upright to maintain its balance.

This sword-billed hummingbird is adapted to feeding on nectar from plants with extremely long corolla tubes, giving it a competitive advantage. However, one disadvantage is that the bill is useless for preening. Instead, the feathers must be maintained by scratching with the feet.

This bird goes trap-lining, visiting flowers repeatedly in sequence like a gardener tending his vegetables. Resides in montane forests of the Andes from Venezuela to Bolivia.

ORTOLAN BUNTING
Emberiza hortulana

In a Roman Osteria (1866) by Carl Bloch highlights the sinful pleasure of eating this small and increasingly rare bird. A summer visitor to Europe and Central Asia, the ortolan bunting winters patchily in Sahelian zone of Africa.

This attractive bird may well have remained relatively obscure but for a strange cultural quirk: it is a renowned French delicacy and has been since Roman times. Ortolan buntings were captured on their autumn migration, lured into a cage by another of their kind, and taken alive. They were then blinded, force fed and kept in the dark for several weeks, before being drowned in Armagnac brandy and cooked. Traditionally, the bodies were then eaten whole while the diner kept a napkin over their head, apparently to keep the rich aroma from escaping.

The centuries-old practice has been maintained in a few parts of France, despite the birds being legally protected since 1999, and up to 50,000 birds are still killed each year. With a dramatic recent decline in population, hopefully this barbaric culinary disgrace will soon disappear.

The late French president François Mitterrand chose ortolan for his last meal in 1996.

MERLIN
Falco columbarius

A male (top) and female merlin. These are popular falconry birds found in Eurasian and North American moorland and tundra; they winter further south.

You can often tell whether a merlin is around long before you see it. Birds will flee in panic in all directions, and you might just catch sight of a dashing shape scything through the melée.

A classic merlin hunting technique is known as an exhaustion flight. The predator will latch on to a songbird, tailgating it as it twists and turns and dodges in an effort to escape. These chases may be prolonged, sometimes lasting many minutes. A common quarry in this tense chase would be a skylark in Europe or a horned lark in North America; but by no means do all end in the merlin's favour.

AQUATIC WARBLER
Acrocephalus paludicola

This rare bird of bogs and marshes in east and central European is now highly protected; migrates to West Africa just south of Sahara.

Conservationists can be ingenious. The aquatic warbler is a very rare songbird that is now confined to Poland, Belarus and Ukraine. In the winter it migrates to Africa, but until recently nobody knew where.

Scientists are aware that every part of the world has a distinct geochemical profile of stable isotopes. These chemicals are everywhere and leave an imprint in a bird's environment, including the food that it eats. As a bird grows its feathers, the isotope profile is preserved.

A conservation team, knowing that aquatic warblers grow their tail feathers while at their wintering grounds, caught some individuals, snipped off a few millimetres of feathers and analyzed them. Meanwhile, fieldworkers in West Africa, where the bird was suspected to winter, gathered the isotope profiles from the resident birds of a number of different regions.

The isotope detectives narrowed down the search, and in 2007 the birds were duly found, in Senegal.

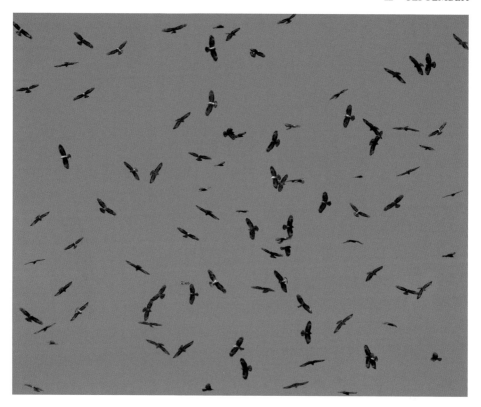

HONEY BUZZARD
Pernis apivorus

The only known predator of the Asian giant hornet is not after honey but wasps and other stinging insects. The honey buzzard breeds in high summer in forests of Europe and western Asia; migrates in September to sub-Saharan Africa.

The honey buzzard is a strange raptor which is a summer visitor to Eurasia. Chief among its curious habits is its diet, which consists mainly of wasps and their grubs, as well as other stinging insects. The birds spend the day watching wasps come and go, and eventually raid their nests. The raptor has strong, but not especially sharp claws to break the nests, and it has stiffened feathers on its face to protect it against stings.

After breeding, honey buzzards migrate to Africa for the winter, and one of the grandest sights in European birding is to see streams of them pass by at this time of year, spiralling overhead. The migration is quick, and the birds fast during most of their journey.

SWAINSON'S HAWK
Buteo swainsoni

These hawks often wait and watch for prey from a high viewpoint or take advantage of farming activity to scare out small creatures. They breed in the high plains of central western North America, with a remarkable migration to the plains of Argentina, Paraguay and southern Brazil.

This lovely hawk of the North America Great Plains is the ultimate in migratory raptors. At the end of summer, after breeding in North America, the population flies all the way to Argentina, a distance of at least 10,000km (over 6,000 miles). They are famous for travelling in flocks, sometimes several thousand strong, and riding thermals, which form over warm ground and rise up. The birds use these air masses and appear as if they are climbing an invisible spiral staircase, and the sight of many birds all soaring in the same thermal is called a 'kettle'. Watching a large kettle is a thrilling sight indeed.

The birds change their diet prior to migration. During breeding they eat rodents and other small mammals and feed these to their young. By August, however, they switch to insects such as grasshoppers. Eating large amounts of swarming insects enables them to fatten up suitably for their long journey that they begin around now.

OILBIRD
Steatornis caripensis

A cave dweller of evergreen lowland and montane forests in northern and western South America.

Some birds live niche lifestyles, and this is one of them. Oilbirds are the only birds in the world that are nocturnal fruit-eaters. They are also the only birds, apart from a few swifts, that use echolocation to move around in the dark. It isn't as sophisticated as a bat's super-sense, but oilbirds nest in caves in the pitch black, so they need it.

Every night members of a colony fly out of the cave and commute to fruiting trees, sometimes covering an area of 40km (25 miles) or more. They strip what they need from the treetops and then return, again as a group. The young grow up on a diet of regurgitated fruit, and they will eat nothing else for the rest of their lives. Oilbird caves stink, and are covered with pips, seeds and rotting fruit; even the nest is partly made up of pulp. The diet is short on protein, and the youngsters take a long time to develop, but they eventually become enormously fat. Unfortunately, this sometimes can be their downfall, as local people kill them and use their fluids as cooking oil.

GALAPAGOS MOCKINGBIRD
Mimus parvulus

Found on most islands of the Galapagos and in many habitats.

This was the day in 1835 on which Charles Darwin's experience on the Galapagos Islands began, when the crew of HMS *Beagle* sighted San Cristóbal island. He left the archipelago just over a month later. His short visit was crucial in developing his theory of evolution by natural selection, so you could say it turned the scientific world upside down.

The popular impression of Darwin on the Galapagos is that it was the finches, each with a different bill shape, that most intrigued the scientist. This isn't true at all; Darwin paid little attention to the dull, blackish birds. It was the mockingbirds that really interested him, and he collected many from different islands and compared them. Aside from the widespread Galapagos mockingbird, there are three other species, some found on only one island.

SPOON-BILLED SANDPIPER
Calidris pygmaea

Still hunted, and with its habitat thoughtlessly destroyed, this sandpiper is on the edge of extinction.

It is always a tragedy when a bird is most famous for being endangered. This is especially true when it's unique. The spoon-billed sandpiper is the only wader with a spatulate bill, which it uses to swish from side to side, in the manner of – well, a spoonbill.

The plight of this tiny shorebird has become a conservation *cause célèbre*, partly because it is such a singular delight. There are almost certainly fewer than 500 left, with a terrifying rate of decline of 26 per cent annually. So critical is the situation that extreme measures have been taken to protect it, including captive breeding.

The spoon-billed sandpiper is a little fussy: for its breeding habitat in north-east Asia it needs vegetated lagoon-spits close to an estuary; and for the rest of the time it needs sandy tidal flats with very shallow water. To protect it, you need to preserve its breeding grounds, wintering grounds and anywhere it needs for refuelling in between.

GREATER ROADRUNNER
Geococcyx californianus

At up to 26mph (32kmh), the roadrunner really does run, but is also spends a lot of time resting in the shade. It is native to the arid scrubby country of southern USA and northern Mexico.

It was on this day in 1949 that a series of cartoons brought a relatively obscure bird to the world's attention. The endless story of Wile E. Coyote's attempts to catch and eat the Road Runner is told in a number of shorts from the Looney Tunes and Merrie Melodies stable, which are still frequently shown on TV around the world. The plot resembles the world famous *Tom and Jerry* cartoons: cat never catches mouse and the coyote never catches the roadrunner, despite all the misadventures.

People are sometimes surprised to learn that there really is a roadrunner, although its call is not 'Beep, beep' as in the cartoons. It is actually a stripy, long-tailed member of the cuckoo family found in the southern United States and Mexico. It really does run along the ground and down roads. It has an impressive and varied diet, including snakes, scorpions, millipedes, spiders and other desert goodies.

As far as is known, the coyote is not a frequent natural enemy.

MALLARD
Anas platyrhynchos

Worldwide as a domestic duck. Native in all kinds of wetlands in Eurasia and North America; introduced to Australasia.

If you have ever eaten duck, the chances are it was this one. It has been domesticated for around 3,500 years in both China and Europe. If you've eaten Peking duck, that's still a mallard, despite being large and white and nothing like the ancestral form. Unusually for a domesticated animal, wild, authentic versions are still abundant. However, on your local lake you might well see all manner of strangely coloured ducks, none of which looks quite the same as the others – these are genetic experiments writ semi-wild. Many have different calls to wild mallards, and different behaviour, but they are derived from the same stock.

Ducks are famous for their call, but the distinctive belly-laugh of hysterical quacking is always made by females. Males quack softly, and also make a series of whistles.

RING-NECKED DOVE
Streptopelia capicola

Found in any open habitat across eastern and southern Africa, and often congregating at waterholes, these birds are the sound of Africa.

You might not have heard of this bird, but you've definitely heard its call; the three simple notes form the acoustic backdrop to just about every African safari documentary and feature film. It doesn't matter what the film is about, whether it's lions, elephants or people, the ring-necked dove is sure to be there in the background, its voice redolent of the hot, dusty African bush.

INDIAN ROLLER
Coracias benghalensis

Common in open country in India and Sri Lanka west to Arabia, this bird mainly eats beetles and crickets.

The rollers are a small group of colourful medium-sized birds that sport a range of blue and purplish hues. They live in open country where they use a hunting technique called 'perch and pounce'. For this they choose an elevated lookout point to scan the ground below, where they hope a large invertebrate such as a beetle or centipede might wander past. When it spots something, the roller pounces, grabbing the unfortunate creature in its powerful bill.

In some parts of India this species is considered sacred as a representation of the god Shiva. In other parts of that same country it is cooked in a broth and served as a cure for a cough, presumably a reference to the bird's harsh voice.

COMMON BARN OWL
Tyto alba

Found in almost every region, this hunter could find you in complete darkness – and you wouldn't hear it coming. Good thing you're not a vole.

With its ghostly white plumage, silent flight and heart-shaped face, the barn owl seems like an ethereal, alien creature – and the reality is even stranger. For this extraordinary predator can catch prey in total darkness, using only its ears to detect it – provided its target – a mouse or a vole – is making sufficient noise. One of the barn owl's ears, the left one, is fitted slightly higher up vertically on the side of its head than its right one, making the ear openings asymmetrical. This means that sound coming from above or below will arrive at the upper ear at a fractionally different time to the lower ear, and the owl processes the time difference. At the same time, as in the case of our own ears, sound coming from the horizontal plane arrives at the ear on the right at a fractionally different time to the ear on the left. Together, these time differentials are calculated by the owl's brain to give a three-dimensional directional reading, based on the sound alone.

"Kenn-Ken-Ken..." "Green Woodpecker"

EURASIAN GREEN WOODPECKER
Picus viridis

Lives in woodland glades and open areas in temperate Europe east to Afghanistan.

This is a woodpecker that is as much at home on the ground as it is in the trees; the green plumage provides a clue. Its main diet, accounting for the majority of its food, comprises ants of multiple species. It can often be seen on lawns in gardens and parks, feeding on colonial ants in the soil. The bird uses its bill to dig funnel-shaped boreholes into the ground, fracturing the ants' subterranean hideaways, allowing it to lap up the colony members with its sticky, wide-tipped tongue fed by an enlarged salivary gland.

A woodpecker's tongue is extraordinary. It is so long that, when not extended, the hyoid apparatus must curve around the top of the skull to accommodate it. The tongue of the green woodpecker protrudes 10cm (4in) beyond the tip of the bill.

BLACK-CAPPED CHICKADEE
Poecile atricapillus

Common resident of gardens and forests in central and northern North America.

In many modern human cultures, both sexism and ageism are frowned upon. In black-capped chickadee society, they are part of life.

In the winter, when most North Americans are enjoying the antics of chickadees on the backyard bird feeder, these birds are found in stable parties of 3–12 individuals. Within this grouping there is a strict hierarchy, which may play out when individuals bicker over food, for example. In these hierarchies, males are always dominant over females, and older birds are dominant over younger ones.

In the following breeding season, the hierarchies play out in a similar way as birds leave the flock and nest as separate pairs. Invariably, older, more experienced males pair up the quickest, and are the most sought after. These same old rogues also take part in more copulations, not just with their mates, but also with other females that are interested in investing in some good DNA. In the bird world, older is better – and sexier.

CHINESE HWAMEI
Garrulax canorus

Also called the melodious laughingthrush, this bird is resident in woodland and thicket in China, Vietnam and Laos; widely introduced, including to Hawaii.

For thousands of years, the hwamei has been a fixture as a cage bird in China. Although undoubtedly attractive – the name means 'painted eyebrow' – the main reason is its loud, melodious song, which is a rich, varied soliloquy with some repetition and a good many imitations of other birds. Breeders have long entered their birds for competitions, in which a great deal of money is at stake. A talented hwamei can still make its owner rich. A more sinister activity exploits the territorial disposition of the male hwamei: people would sometimes put two males in such close proximity that they would fight – a songbird version of a cock fight.

Thankfully the bird is still common in many parts of China.

INDIGO BUNTING
Passerina cyanea

Some classic experiments on indigo buntings in the 1960s confirmed something wonderful – that birds can orientate using the stars. It turns out that they observe the rotation of the firmament around the North Star in order to find where south is, just as people can do.

What is truly amazing, though, is that birds have to learn how to do this. Indigo buntings hand-reared in a planetarium projection with most of the stars missing from around the North Pole were found not to be able to orientate. Conversely, birds hand-reared in a planetarium projection with a natural sky flew in the right direction. Youngsters reared in a planetarium where the night sky was reversed 180 degrees tried to fly north in the autumn instead of south.

The birds learn the rotation of the sky during their early days; perhaps while still in the nest.

A summer visitor to brushy areas in eastern North America, the indigo bunting migrates about now to Central America and Caribbean.

EUROPEAN GOLDFINCH
Carduelis carduelis

Weedy fields
in Europe,
western Asia
and around the
Mediterranean;
northern
populations
migrate south
in winter.

One millimetre is all it takes. One millimetre determines a lifestyle and separates the sexes.

The European goldfinch is a seed-eater with a particular attachment to thistles. Up to one-third of its annual diet consists of thistle seeds, as well as those of other plants. Its young are brought up on seed broth.

Another favourite food is the teasel, which produces its seeds at a similar time, in the autumn. This plant is also tall, with spines. The flower head is protected by a covering of spiny bracts. It so happens that the seeds are harder for a female goldfinch to reach than for a male, because the latter's bill is one millimetre longer. That millimetre sets males out on a search for teasels, leaving some of the precious thistle crop to the females.

ARCTIC TERN
Sterna paradisaea

Breeding across Arctic and boreal lakes and tundra in Eurasia and North America, the Arctic tern is migrating to the Antarctic at the moment, to wander the oceans there.

The Arctic tern's claim to fame is that it has the longest migratory journey in the world. It could hardly fly much further. Many birds breed well north of the Arctic Circle, and then migrate south to the Antarctic in winter, spanning much of the globe from north to south. Once in the Southern Oceans they don't necessarily stop, but instead some make a circumnavigation of the Antarctic continent, in search of fish stocks. Recent radio-tracking has revealed migratory distances of 70,000–90,000km (43,500 miles–56,000 miles) annually, far more than any other bird.

As a migrant that goes from extreme north to extreme south, the Arctic tern also presumably sees more daylight per year than any other creature.

EURASIAN NUTHATCH
Sitta europaea

At home in deciduous and mixed woods of Europe, northern Asia, China and Japan.

Many birds throughout the world earn a living by climbing tree limbs and searching the bark closely for the treasure trove of invertebrates that hide away in the fissures, cracks and imperfections. Nuthatches, though, are very unusual for their ability, not just to climb up trunks and branches, but also to climb down head-first. They do so by holding one foot above the other, using the top foot as an anchor and the lower foot as a pivot. Presumably, the ability to look down the tree trunks, at an angle that a woodpecker, for example, could not see, gives them a competitive advantage in finding food.

BLUE
BIRD-OF-PARADISE
Paradisornis rudolphi

Could this be the pinnacle of the bird world? Would seeing the blue bird-of-paradise be the ultimate in birding experiences?

This marvel has flair, it has charisma. It is stunning beyond belief. It is striking in the pattern and shape of its gorgeous plumage. It occurs in the tropical forests of New Guinea, haunt of many dream birds. It is hard to find, giving a dose of drama to the search.

And could there be a more extraordinary courtship display? The male ruffles its feathers and then hangs upside down like a bat, wagging his body up and down so that the cobalt-blue flank plumes shimmer and cascade like the train of a wedding dress. At the same time, he produces the strangest buzzing sound, like the throb of an electric motor.

Indeed, the effect is electrifying. The bird is electrifying. The world is wondrous.

The blue feathers on this headdress of a Jika tribal dancer are from the blue bird-of-paradise. Found in forests of Papua New Guinea (see also photograph page 368).

GREATER COUCAL
Centropus sinensis

Breeding and calling now in many parts of southern Asia.

This is a cuckoo, but not as you know it. The greater coucal is a *bona fide* member of the same family as the common cuckoo, but – headline news – it builds its own nest, lays its own eggs and raises its own chicks. In fact, only about one-third of species in the cuckoo family are parasitic on other birds, with the majority being 'blameless'.

Mind you, the greater coucal does build an awful nest: a large globe with a side entrance, incompetently assembled from grass and palm fronds.

Its song is deep and cuckoo-like; a splendid series of deep, glugging notes which accelerate a little, the rhythm similar to that made by pouring water out of a bottle.

275

BLACK SKIMMER
Rynchops niger

A black skimmer skimming. Found on sheltered coasts of eastern North America; widespread on wetlands in South America.

You only have to look at the bill of a skimmer to guess that there is something unusual about the way it feeds. The lower mandible is always longer than the upper mandible (maxilla) and it is compressed laterally, like a knife.

The bird feeds by flying very low so that its lower mandible slices through the water's surface. When the lower mandible touches a fish, the maxilla immediately snaps shut around it, and the head and neck duck downwards to secure the catch. Fish caught in this way are usually 3–12cm (1–5in) long.

Remarkably, the skimmer has no other feeding method. Well, with a bill like that, it couldn't really do much else!

COMMON STONECHAT
Saxicola torquatus

Open country with bushes in much of the Old World, including Eurasia and Africa; many populations in the north migrate south in winter.

A birdwatcher's favourite, the stonechat is one of those rarities: a bird that keeps still long enough to be identified and admired. That's not a coincidence, because sitting upright on a perch, surveying the scene, is the stonechat's core feeding method. By using elevated vantage points, a stonechat can monitor the comings and goings of the invertebrates that it eats, be they on the ground, crawling in the grass, or even bumbling past in flight. Once a tasty morsel has been spotted, all the stonechat needs to do is fly towards it and catch it in its bill. A working stonechat, on average, changes perch every 25 seconds.

The stonechat's open perches allow it to be highly vigilant, and it is extremely effective at spotting danger. In fact, it is so good that other birds will stay close to the stonechat when they are foraging themselves. A particular nuisance is the Dartford warbler, which can hang on a stonechat's tail for hours, but other birds do it too.

RUDDY TURNSTONE
Arenaria interpres

Breeds in tundra across the Arctic; winters on rocky coasts almost worldwide.

This is a small, dumpy shorebird that is usually found among rocks and seaweed, at least in the autumn and winter. Its English common name is derived from the habit of using its sharp bill and powerful neck muscles to overturn stones and other items to reveal what might be edible underneath.

Turnstones take the term 'edible' to its limit. Birds have been known to feast contentedly on soap. They are also among the few birds known to eat a human corpse. More typically, they feed on a wide variety of rockpool inhabitants, including starfish, worms, crustaceans, molluscs and insects.

A bird closely associated with beds of common reed across temperate Europe and Asia. Here, the male bird is shown at the top, the female beneath him.

BEARDED REEDLING
Panurus biarmicus

A charismatic bird of extensive reedbeds in Eurasia, the strikingly coloured bearded reedling is not closely related to any other bird in the world. It is strongly tied to its habitat, feeding on the seeds of reeds and other wetland plants in the autumn and winter, and on caterpillars and other insects in the reeds in the spring and summer. It is rarely ever found anywhere else.

In autumn, however, the bearded reedling does sometimes move out of its home reed bed in a bid to colonise elsewhere. Departures are signalled by a delightful display known as 'high flying'. These normally secretive birds suddenly fly up vertically into the air, often to 10m (33ft) or more, giving their distinctive, pinging calls. Usually they drop back into the reeds, but every so often a couple will rise higher and higher and begin their journey to pastures new.

ALGERIAN NUTHATCH
Sitta ledanti

Like other nuthatches, this bird can walk up a tree and then down head first. It lives in mountain oak forests in four locations in northern Algeria.

To discover a new species is one of the great thrills and privileges of life. It doesn't happen to many of us. True, you can study leaf moulds or flatworms and you might make a discovery every week, but the Holy Grail of exploration is now to find a new bird or mammal.

You can be quite sure that, on the morning of 5 October 1975, Jean-Paul Ledant, a young Belgian, would not have even begun to entertain such thoughts. For one thing, he was on a forestry expedition; for another, he was at the Djebel Babor nature reserve in Algeria, and northern Africa already had a long history of exploration, particularly of birds. But on that afternoon, as he settled down to write, Ledant heard a tapping sound and, looking up, saw a nuthatch. Although he thought there was something interesting about it, it was only when his colleagues back home told him that there were no nuthatches in Algeria that everyone realized this was a little more than just interesting. It was a sensation.

However, they decided against releasing the news until they could return to the site and collect more information, which proved to be difficult. In the meantime, in June 1976, a Swiss naturalist called Eric Brunier independently visited Djebel Babor unaware of the discovery. He duly stumbled upon the nuthatch and, for a short while thought that he had made the first sensational find. Sadly, for him, he was eight months too late.

Many people would have been devastated to miss out on such an accolade. Incredibly, though, in 1988, Eric Brunier went to Tanzania to work as a medical doctor and – you've guessed it – he stumbled upon a new species of bird. Well, actually it was three …

RUBY-THROATED HUMMINGBIRD
Archilochus colubris

Familiar to many in eastern North America, this hummer visits thousands of backyard feeders right up into southern Canada. Its remarkable migration takes it to Central America. When it reaches the Gulf Coast, some ruby-throated hummingbirds simply fly across the Gulf of Mexico to the Yucatan Peninsula, which involves a 20-hour flight non-stop for at least 800km (500 miles). In order to perform this miraculous feat, they double their body weight, bingeing on nectar.

TAWNY OWL
Strix aluco

Then nightly sings the staring owl,
'Tu-whit;
Tu-who', a merry note ...

So wrote the great English playwright William Shakespeare in *Love's Labour's Lost*, written in 1595. The wondrous, haunting, quavering hoot of the tawny owl still causes shivers down the spine over the owl's range.

Many people assume that it is only the male that makes the sound described above. However, the 'Tu-whit' call is made by both sexes.

Above: Inhabits
larger forests of
south-east Asia,
Malay peninsula,
Java and parts
of India.

Top left: A
visitor to
backyard
hummingbird
feeders as
far north as
southern Canada.

Bottom left:
Common
woodland and
garden owl
calling now in
Europe, west
Asia and
North Africa.

GREAT HORNBILL
Buceros bicornis

It seems too big for a forest bird. Huge, it flies with a swish of the wings so loud that it could be a misplaced swan. King of the treetops, the hornbill lives an arboreal life eating high-hanging fruit and small animals.

Hornbills have an extraordinary behavioural quirk. During the breeding season, the female is kept in a nesting chamber in the hole of a forest giant, with only a narrow slit-shaped window to look out of. It is a voluntary incarceration; the female plays her part in narrowing the hole entrance with mud, excreta and food remains. Once 'imprisoned', she, her eggs and subsequent nestlings depend on rations brought in by the hard-working, foraging male. The female uses the narrow window for receiving food deliveries, and for defaecating outwards. While on duty, the female makes use of her time by moulting her feathers.

After 3-4 months, the female, and usually sometime later the young, break out of the nest hole, having been kept from harm by their wall of mud.

RUFOUS HORNERO
Furnarius rufus

Favours open country in warmer lowlands of eastern and southern South America.

It takes a lot for a dull brown nonentity to become the national bird of both Argentina and Uruguay, but the rufous hornero has done so through sheer force of personality. A bird of open scrubland, it is abundant throughout pastoral land in southern South America and reaches into suburbia. Its signature trait, though, is its remarkable nest, which is known by everyone. It is made of mud, fashioned into a round structure that resembles an old-style adobe oven, giving rise to the local name *el hornero*, the baker.

The nest is 20–30cm (8–12in) in diameter and 20–25cm (8–10in) high and is built by the breeding pair over a busy couple of weeks. According to a delightful local piece of folklore, the builders rest from their efforts on Sundays. The structures are never reused by their creators, and soon become refuges for a wide range of other wildlife, which includes other birds, lizards and small rodents.

BLACKPOLL WARBLER
Setophaga striata

Inhabitant of the northernmost coniferous forests of North America, this warbler migrates to winter in northern South America.

O h, to sit on the back of a blackpoll warbler during its autumn migration! The things you would see and experience if you were following it right now.

This tiny bird sets out from its breeding grounds across northern North America and, rather than following the coasts, takes the shortest route, flying right out over the Atlantic Ocean and down past Bermuda. The prevailing winds then shift to north-easterlies, which guide it to the shores of the Caribbean islands. This journey necessitates making a single flight over the deep ocean lasting for 3,000km (nearly 2,000 miles), and potential 88 hours of non-stop flying. Even then the blackpoll warbler hasn't finished, continuing on an unknown route down to northern South America.

EURASIAN JAY
Garrulus glandarius

This chatty acorn-lover favours woodlands of temperate Europe and Asia, east to Japan.

There is no easier time than now to see the jay, an otherwise shy bird of woodlands in Europe and Asia. In the summer, jays disappear into the canopy, but now they are everywhere, flying to and fro with their curiously unsteady flight, passing over houses and shops and thoroughfares.

It's because autumn is the time to collect acorns for their winter stores. And they do it in style. Each pair or individual has a territory, and their focus is to stack their house full of long-lasting fruit. If there are no oak trees nearby, they must commute to find them, even if the stands are several kilometres away. These journeys can fill an entire day in October.

The acorns are then hidden away, one by one, each in a different place – on the ground here, in the bark of a tree there. The jay remembers where all or most of them are. A neglected store can become a mighty oak tree.

At the end of the collecting season a pair of jays might have collected 5,000 acorns in all – an ample emergency food supply.

NORTHERN HOUSE MARTIN
Delichon urbicum

Nests on buildings and cliffs throughout Europe and western Asia; migrates south to unknown parts of Africa.

For the moment at least, it remains one of the great mysteries of bird migration. Where does the house martin, a bird that builds a cup out of mud on many millions of human dwellings, go in the winter? Everybody knows it goes to Africa, but so far only a few flocks of just hundreds of birds have been seen across a broad swathe of sub-Saharan Africa. Bearing in mind that the European population is at least 30 million pairs, there are a lot of 'lost' birds somewhere in the African heartland.

As October closes in, the birds go south; one moment they are on our walls and ledges, the next they are flying to a mysterious destination.

PALM COCKATOO
Probosciger aterrimus

This drummer
boy's natural
habitat is in
the rainforests
of northern
Australia and
New Guinea.

Everybody has heard of woodpeckers using their bills to drum noisily on trees, making familiar, rapid taps. One species of bird in the world does the same thing, but uses a drumstick instead.

The palm cockatoo of New Guinea and northern Australia fashions a special instrument out of wood, using its powerful bill. The bird then takes the drumstick in one foot and bangs out a rhythm against a favoured hollow trunk.

At present, nobody knows why it does this.

BAR-HEADED GOOSE
Anser indicus

A high-flyer that breeds in the mountain lakes of Central Asia, mainly Tibet and migrates over the Himalayas to lowland southern Asia.

The bar-headed goose doesn't look special, but it makes the highest-altitude regular migration of any bird on the planet around this time of year, flying from the mountain lakes of central Asia to lowland India, China and Myanmar. Those that fly to northern India pass over the Himalayas, sometimes at heights well above that of Mount Everest, at 8,848m (over 29,000ft).

This is an exceptional feat and requires a number of adaptations. Bar-headed geese have larger lungs than other birds of their size and have comparatively more blood capillaries in their heart. They have a special form of haemoglobin, which allows them to extract a greater amount of oxygen at low pressures. They even have a unique enzyme to help with energy production in some of their muscle cells.

Other than that, they are just normal geese.

REDWING
Turdus iliacus

Many birds around the world are celebrated as heralds of spring; rather fewer are appreciated as harbingers of winter.

One that is, though, is the redwing. This handsome thrush is an abundant northern breeder, and cascades down south to winter in many parts of Europe and Asia. One of the events of autumn here is to step outside on a frosty, starry night, and hear the 'seep' call of a redwing. The noise betrays the presence of an army of birds flying overhead, with winter on their tails.

HAWFINCH
Coccothraustes coccothraustes

The outsize bill of the hawfinch has evolved to crack the toughest of seeds, those unavailable to other competitors. The mandibles can exert a crushing force of 45kg (100lb), equivalent to the weight of two bags allowed on an international flight! The hawfinch has no trouble with cherry stones and olives, among other seeds. It is a Eurasian species particularly fond of oak, hornbeam and beech woods.

TAWNY FROGMOUTH
Podargus strigoides

It looks like an owl and comes out at night, but Australia's tawny frogmouth is an entirely different bird, lacking an owl's talons, and with a much wider bill gape, no less than 5cm (2in) in a bird that is 34–53cm (13–21in) in length. It feeds by flying down from an elevated perch on to a range of small animals and simply grabbing them in its bill. Prey items include moths, spiders, worms, scorpions, wasps, centipedes and slugs, making the frogmouth a welcome guest in many Australian suburban gardens.

By the day, the frogmouth's extraordinary camouflage makes it almost impossible to spot.

Left: Sitting in an Australian gum tree, the tawny frogmouth is excellently camouflaged.

Opposite, top: Arctic and boreal wood and scrub across Eurasia; winters in western and central Europe, North Africa and south-west Asia.

Left bottom: At home in the forests of Europe, North Africa and parts of temperate Asia.

291

SOOTY TERN
Onychoprion fuscatus

Above: A sooty tern breeding colony.

Top right: Common across Eurasia from Europe to Japan.

Bottom right: A bird of Central America and northern South America, south to Bolivia.

A great deal of mystery surrounds the life of the sooty tern. It is a sea bird that breeds on tropical islands around the globe, often in large, dense colonies. Away from the breeding sites, though, it wanders widely over the oceans. Remarkably, once they leave the colony, the young birds spend 2–5 years at sea before returning. They probably stay aloft for the entire time, because they don't have waterproof plumage and, other than the odd bit of flotsam, there is nowhere to perch and rest. They must sleep on the wing.

Sooty terns often spend much of their time following hunting packs of tuna or other large, predatory fish. They feed by snatching smaller fish that leap out of the water to evade capture.

CARRION CROW
Corvus corone

Crows are among the most intelligent of all birds, and there are many examples of their ingenuity. Carrion crows in some Japanese cities have taken to dropping large nuts on to busy roads, so the shells are flattened by car tyres. Retrieving the smashed nuts can be dangerous, so the crows have opted for the strategy of dropping them just beyond pedestrian crossings. They then wait patiently for the lights to turn red and the traffic to stop before flying down to claim their prize.

SPOTTED BARBTAIL
Premnoplex brunnescens

Tropical forests are renowned for their panoply of birds of dazzling colours and glorious, showy patterns. But there remain, in those same forests, a substantial cohort of modestly coloured counterparts, largely neglected, but fascinating and often poorly known. Such is the spotted barbtail. This attractive bird is confined to upland mossy forests, usually above 1,000m (3,300ft) in elevation, where it forages on tree bark for invertebrates, usually low down. Today, let's hear it for the birds of the underworld.

AUSTRALIAN BRUSH-TURKEY
Alectura lathami

A baby Australian brush-turkey can fly as soon as his feathers are dry.

We all know that birds reproduce by laying eggs and then sitting tight to incubate them.

Except sometimes they don't. There is a group of birds in Australia and Polynesia called the megapodes ('bigfeet'), which have a quite different strategy. They use an external incubator, not their own bodies.

The male Australian brush-turkey gathers substantial amounts of leaves and other litter and constructs an earthen mound about 1m (3¼ft) high and anything up to 4m (13ft) across. Inside this mound, the leaves and other material begins to decompose and create heat. It is this heat that incubates the eggs.

It isn't quite as straightforward as it sounds, because to ensure the eggs hatch, the male needs to keep the temperature inside the mound constant at 33–35°C (around 93°F), for up to ten months. This involves adding or removing earth or leaves, and it seems that the brush-turkey has a built-in thermometer, as it tests the heat by inserting its bill. It might need to add material during the cool of the morning and take it away during the heat of the day.

A dominant male is in charge of a mound and keeps other males away, while the females of the neighbourhood come and go, mating with the male and depositing eggs in his mound. There may well be 20 using it at one time.

All in all, it is far more labour-intensive than just sitting on eggs!

GREATER RACQUET-TAILED DRONGO
Dicrurus paradiseus

With such a name you might not believe it exists, but the greater racket-tailed drongo is alive and well across a broad swathe of southern Asia. Drongos are a family of medium-sized, crow-like black birds of forests and clearings, all with loud and variable voices.

Along with other drongos, this species spends much of its time in mixed feeding flocks, which are a feature of many forests of the world. Multiple species flock together, all foraging for different items, but keeping together for safety purposes. And drongos are professional sentinels. They perch above the feeding flock, keeping a lookout for danger, and when it appears, they make a loud alarm call. Cleverly, they don't just make their own alarm calls, but imitate those of others in the flock.

Sometimes, though, when hungry, they just give a false alarm instead, when no danger is present. Feeding birds scatter and often drop edible items as they flee, and these the drongo snatches. It cannot give too many false alarms, though, because other birds will start to ignore them, so it must be sparing.

Forest and gardens of southern Asia, from India east to south-east Asia and Sundas.

AUSTRALIAN SWAMPHEN
Porphyrio melanotus

These libertine birds of Australia, New Zealand, New Guinea and many islands work as a group to bring up the young.

These birds are purple, bulky, chicken-like and noisy. They have an outsize frontal shield and bill, both of which are scarlet. Their legs are lanky and pink and used for running and gripping vegetation. But despite their distinctive appearance, swamphens are most remarkable for their 'anything goes' breeding behaviour.

You name it – polygamy, homosexuality, incest – the Australasian swamphen will do it at one time or another. Some pairs breed monogamously, but others come together in multiple groups of males and females. The females all lay in the same nest, which may hold up to 18 eggs, while the males maintain territory and incubate. Everyone feeds the chicks and everyone defends the borders. Skirmishes with neighbouring groups may be violent. If the sex ratio skews too much, homosexual bonds are common. Since many in each group are related and may be previous offspring of a pair in the same group, incest is inevitable.

JAPANESE CORMORANT
Phalacrocorax capillatus

Ogata Kenzan's 1743 painting captures the ancient Japanese art of *ukai*, or cormorant fishing. The cormorants breed on the rocky coasts of Japan and nearby mainland China and Korea; they winter more widely in neighbouring east Asia.

The Japanese cormorant is found on the coasts of eastern Asia, particularly in Japan, as its English common name implies. Here it is known as *umi-u*, the sea cormorant, and it is famous for being used in the ancient practice of cormorant fishing (*ukai*) where a cormorant master (*usho*) manages cormorants to help catch fish. In some parts of Japan, such as the Nagara River, this symbiosis between bird and human has been going on for more than 1,000 years.

Cormorants are supreme immersion-hunters, catching fish in an underwater chase. The tame individuals use their skills, but the fishermen fix a ring across the throat so that their charges cannot swallow the larger catches. The cormorant surfaces, the men bring the tethered bird in and extract the larger fish from the throat of the bird. The cormorant is able to swallow smaller fish and will also be allowed a share of the spoils.

Remarkably, *ukai* was once an industry, but is now a tourist attraction.

GROOVE-BILLED ANI
Crotophaga sulcirostris

Lives in the understorey of scrub, gardens, open forests in extreme southern USA, Central America and north-west South America.

This is a member of the cuckoo family but the behaviour of this bird is extraordinary. It is almost as if a groove-billed ani had read a book about the exploits of its famous relative, the parasitic common cuckoo and decided 'I'm going to do everything differently.'

Thus, not only does the groove-billed ani build a nest, lay its own eggs and raise its own young, it does this communally. Groups of anis, consisting of up to five pairs, make a joint nest, with all birds contributing to the building. Each of the females lays eggs in the nest, creating a clutch of up to 20 eggs. Thereafter, the group shares incubation and feeding duties, to bring up the young together. It is as if this was a hippie commune trying to atone for the sins of the family to which the members belong.

They say a leopard doesn't change its spots, though. Sometimes, when a female comes to the nest to lay an egg, she removes one belonging to a co-nester and disposes of it.

EASTERN WHIPBIRD
Psophodes olivaceus

This olive-coloured bird has a call like a slow-motion whip crack. They reside in wet forest and scrub in eastern Australia.

Take a walk any time of year in the forests of eastern Australia, from Queensland south to Victoria, and you are likely to hear a strange sound from the undergrowth. It sounds exactly like the cracking of a whip, with a whistled build-up, and it gives this elusive ground-dwelling bird its English common name. However loud the sound is, try to catch sight of the caller and you are seldom successful, as whipbirds prefer to remain hidden.

Listen closely and you will make out that the whip-crack is only part of the call; there are often other, sounds added on. These are typically made by the female. The pair routinely duet together, to let each other know where they are, since they may forage 20m (66ft) or more apart.

GREY PHALAROPE (RED PHALAROPE)
Phalaropus fulicarius

Breeds on tundra pools of North America, Iceland and eastern Eurasia and winters out to sea in Atlantic and Pacific Oceans.

This bird looks like a toy duck being sucked into a whirlpool, spinning round and round on the spot. Tiny and hyperactive, it gives the impression that a zephyr of wind could whisk it away. Yet the grey phalarope (known as the red phalarope in North America) is a master of the oceans, living far from land for most of the year, eating nothing but zooplankton from the surface. Its true home is the ocean upwellings, where nutrients are brought to the surface by underwater currents, but it is also drawn to the activities of marine mammals such as whales, which are messy feeders, and themselves stir up their own currents. The grey phalarope has been seen picking food directly from an ocean giant's back.

Amazingly, these marine midgets are related to the shorebirds, such as sandpipers and curlews. When breeding, they transform into something more obviously akin to their relatives, living by tundra pools and at times running around on land.

LONG-TAILED SILKY FLYCATCHER
Ptiliogonys caudatus

Only found in Costa Rica and Panama, this bird (a male here) is about the size of a thrush.

Some birds nestle in obscurity; few have heard of this Central American beauty, native to the highlands of Costa Rica and Panama. It is, though, the sort of bird that everybody should know about.

The long-tailed silky flycatcher splits its diet between two food groups: fruit, of which mistletoe is a favourite; and insects, which it can, as its English common name implies, catch in aerial pursuit flight. When seeking food for its young it sometimes performs several catches in one elegant flight. It is a restless bird, which has the most curious habit of never flying in a straight line. Instead, it constantly changes direction, often darting off in a zig-zag for no particular reason. It tends to fly high and fast, and perches aloft, often against the sky.

TOCO TOUCAN
Ramphastos toco

Inhabits forest edges and grassland in Guyanas and parts of Brazil, mainly southern Amazonia.

There's no getting away from it; toucans are famous for their bills. Sometimes you want to describe how someone looks but studiously avoid mentioning the obvious for fear of caricature. But you can't do that with toucans – they are defined by their bills. That of the toco toucan, the largest, comprises 23cm (9in) of the bird's total length of up to 79cm (31in). Although the bills are large and strong, they are much lighter than they look; inside the horny sheath they are mainly hollow, supported by thin internal struts.

As yet there is no definitive known reason for the disproportionate size of their bill. They certainly allow the bird to reach a long way to pick otherwise inaccessible fruits in the South American rainforests where they live; they do make the bird look frightening, allowing it to dominate other frugivorous species; and the size and brightness could be sexually selected. It could be all these reasons.

EURASIAN OYSTERCATCHER
Haematopus ostralegus

Easily identified by their bright beaks and legs and their elegant black plumage, these birds are found in meadows, fields and tundra across Europe and much of Asia; some winter to the south, for example, along African coasts.

You might think that the art of catching shellfish in the mud is a simple one. However, oystercatchers have two main methods, and these are so different that a given population divides into two different teams.

One team is known as stabbers. These birds creep up on an open shellfish and snip the adductor muscle that holds the two shells of a bivalve shut; the cockle or mussel so disabled can then be easily eaten.

The other team is the hammerers. Members rely on strength rather than stealth. They simply grab a shellfish and hammer the shell until they reach the adductor muscle. Their bills are chisel-shaped for this purpose.

These skills are handed down the generations, since young oystercatchers copy their parents. Hammerers do pair up with stabbers, so the young birds may learn both skills.

Found in
association with
game and cattle
in the savannas
of East and
Southern Africa.

RED-BILLED OXPECKER
Buphagus erythrorhynchus

Oxpeckers are the birds that you see in all the wildlife documentaries made in Africa, perched on the hides of large animals such as giraffes and buffalos. They look innocent enough, living on the pests that plague the larger animals. However, they do have a more sinister side: they have a definite predilection for a meal of blood, and are therefore the perfect bird for Halloween.

They are unique among birds for being specialists in eating ticks, which they pull off with their strong bills. However, they particularly favour engorged ticks, which have already had their meal, and they are also drawn to licking the blood from open wounds. Oh, and they eat blood-sucking flies, too. So, while they might be described as consumers of invertebrates, the suspicion is that it's the still-warm red stuff that is the real draw.

As far as is known, no one has ever seen a reflection of an oxpecker in a mirror.

EURASIAN BUZZARD
Buteo buteo

One of the most successful of all Europe's raptors, the buzzard is highly adaptable. It can dive from a great height on to prey, it can ambush and it can even grasp birds in flight. However, it is now November, and, in many parts of this bird's range, the weather is cold and wet. At these times, you can often see buzzards apparently just standing in a field. What are they doing? They are simply wandering over turf, snatching any earthworms that they find at their feet. It wouldn't make the cut in a wildlife documentary, but it is effective.

WATER PIPIT
Anthus spinoletta

When autumn arrives in Europe many birds fly south to escape the rigours of winter.

But the quirky water pipit is flying north instead – in the wrong direction. This bird breeds in the high mountains of central Europe, the Alps, Pyrenees and Carpathians. In the autumn, it does indeed eschew a harsh climate, but only by going downhill, not down south. Some birds migrate instead to the lowlands of Britain and the Low Countries.

Above: Follows ants
in lowland forests,
Central America
and north-west
South America.

Top left: This
bird of prey is
worm hunting. It
can be spotted in
open country with
woods across much
of Europe and
west Asia.

Bottom left: Breeds
on high plateaux
and meadows
in mountains of
Europe and Asia;
winters downhill,
in freshwater
wetlands.

BICOLORED ANTBIRD
Gymnopithys bicolor

Today is International Antbird Appreciation Day. Actually, it isn't really, but the antbirds are a large group of brown birds found in the American tropics, often in deep forest, and they are fascinating enough to deserve more attention than they get. Take the bicolored antbird. This morning it will wake up in its rainforest home and will search out a swarm of army ants. Tomorrow it will do the same, and every subsequent morning after that for its entire life. It is known as an obligate ant follower, because this is the only way it finds food. It doesn't eat the ants themselves, but instead fields the wide variety of small invertebrates that flees the path of the marauding hoards. In each bicolored antbird territory there will always be one or two armies of ants on the move every day of the year.

WHITE-BREASTED NUTHATCH
Sitta carolinensis

Resident in deciduous forests, parks and gardens over much of North America. These birds eat insects when available and store nuts for the winter.

The smart white-breasted nuthatch could be the archetypal all-American bird, since one of its major call-notes is 'Yank, yank'.

At this time of year, this nuthatch should be easy to see on bird feeders throughout North America. Pairs are busily preparing their winter stores of seeds and other items, so they will be paying many visits to backyard food supplies. They cache each seed at a different site. Interestingly, the males usually stash food in between furrows of bark on the main trunk of a tree, while females choose multiple locations. Perhaps that prevents them getting in each other's way, both during storage and during retrieval on a cold winter's day.

CEDAR WAXWING
Bombycilla cedrorum

This sociable North American bird eats berries whole. It sticks to open woodlands, gardens parks and shrubby fields that provide fruit-plants.

The gorgeous cedar waxwing is very unusual among North American birds for being almost a complete frugivore. It eats berries virtually all year round, not least cedar berries – hence the name.

Berry-eating is extremely thirsty work, and cedar waxwings drink prodigiously. In summer, this isn't a problem, since there is usually plenty of water around. In winter, however, in the northern parts of its range, much of the water is frozen.

The cedar waxwing's solution is to drink snow. And, if it is in the mood, it will fly out from its perch and catch snowflakes in the air. Isn't that a delightful thought?

SNOW GOOSE
Anser caerulescens

Breeds in colonies by water above the tree line in Alaska and Canada; winters quite widely in the southern half of the USA and Central America, sometimes in huge flocks.

The English common name of this species, snow goose, is delightfully apt. Not only are these geese white (usually), but they can also arrive in sudden falls. During their spring or autumn migration, many thousands of glinting white bodies can drop from their flightpath high in the sky and tumble down to Earth, skeins haphazardly falling like snowflakes, the only difference being the shrill barking of the animate geese.

These are uber-social geese; you either see thousands or none at all. They breed in colonies on North America's Arctic tundra and then winter in a small number of suitable places. They graze with their feet wet, rooting up vegetation. By night they roost on water, and watching them leave or return in the twilight, with their white bodies stained pink by the setting sun, is one of the great sights of birding.

EURASIAN BULLFINCH
Pyrrhula pyrrhula

Bullfinches aren't just for Christmas – they live in the UK and across Europe and Asia all year round.

The handsome bullfinch is a shy species with soft plumage of pastel colours. In contrast to other finches, it is very quiet, uttering a soft 'Pu' note, and a curious, halting, creaking song.

It is all the more remarkable, then, that for many centuries in Europe, bullfinches were caught and taught to whistle tunes. Their whistles sound exactly like human ones – it is quite eerie.

When bullfinch whistling was at its most popular, during the 19th century, people would make a great deal of money from training young birds. The trade flourished particularly in Germany. Some birds could whistle the '*Deutschlandlied*', the German national anthem, note perfect.

311

JAVA SPARROW
Lonchura oryzivora

A 15th century Ming Dynasty silk painting showing a Java sparrow. Native to Java and Bali in grassland, agricultural areas and towns, these sparrows are now endangered.

At some time in the distant past, somebody in Bali or Java, where this handsome seed-eating bird lives, decided that it would make a good cage bird. The lovely looks, combined with a sweet, chattering song and a gentle disposition, soon made the bird popular. The idea caught on, and Java sparrows were introduced to China as long ago as the 11th century (later they were depicted in Ming Dynasty art) and in Japan in the 17th century, where again they featured in paintings and the decorative arts. Since then, the bird has been introduced to many areas, where it sometimes becomes a pest in rice paddies. It commonly nests on buildings and depends on people. It is a cage bird worldwide.

And yet now, because of this trade, the Java sparrow is classed as Endangered in the only areas where it occurs naturally.

NORTHERN SHOVELER
Spatula clypeata

This widespread bird's distinctive bill gives him a handy feeding advantage. They breed across Eurasia and North America in wetlands, and winter further south, from Europe, Africa, India, Asia and northern South America.

The shoveler is a run-of-the-mill duck with an enormous bill, which dominates its profile and is its defining feature. It has a feeding method quite similar to that of the flamingo, but has none of its glamour.

Its huge bill is broader at the tip to allow water to enter as the bird swims forward. On the sides of the bill both mandibles are fitted with large numbers of comb-like projections called lamellae, which overlap and intermesh. When feeding, the shoveler uses its tongue to force water out through the sides of the bill, where small particles are trapped, and the edible ones eaten. This sieving is so effective that a shoveler can eat 10 per cent of its body weight in a day.

RED-BILLED QUELEA
Quelea quelea

These small, sparrow-like birds, found across much of sub-Saharan Africa, fly in such numbers that they create what is more of a swarm than a flock.

Most people would expect the world's most abundant wild bird to be found worldwide and to be familiar to us all – a feral pigeon, perhaps, or a house sparrow. But no, the only bird whose population probably exceeds one billion individuals is the red-billed quelea, a weaver-bird from sub-Saharan Africa. Single flocks of this super-abundant species may number in the millions.

Queleas are nomadic, wandering over large swathes of Africa following blooms of ephemeral grasses, which only seed after bouts of heavy rainfall. The seeds are highly nutritious and allow the birds to breed quickly. Incubation takes only 9–10 days and fledging 14 days, the young being fed on insects.

If wild grasses run out, queleas can be devastating agricultural pests. A colony in Namibia with five million adults was thought to consume 1,000 tonnes of seeds during its breeding cycle. No wonder these birds are sometimes described as 'feathered locusts'.

SANDERLING
Calidris alba

The sanderling breeds in the high Arctic on barren stony tundra. This long-distance migrant is currently wintering on sandy beaches throughout much of the world.

This is a High Arctic breeding shorebird, but after the summer, it migrates south to many of the sandy beaches of the world. It is a surf dude, running along the beach and dodging breaking waves. As the surf recedes, sanderlings pick small edible animals from the wash, but must then dodge the next incoming wave, something they manage by running very quickly, with their legs whirring. They have lost their hind toe to reduce friction and allow them to run faster.

The sanderling's ability to find food on apparently bare, sandy mud is extraordinary. The touch receptors on their bill are so sensitive that they don't even need to come into contact with a worm or crustacean in order to detect it. They can simply pick up the vibrations of moving prey, even 2cm (almost 1in) away from the animal itself.

AUSTRALIAN MAGPIE
Gymnorhina tibicen

Dick Frizzell's 1987 illustration of Denis Glover's famous poem, which celebrates the song of this common noisy Australian bird (also introduced to New Zealand).

No one who has visited Australia will have failed to hear the extraordinary vocalizations of the Australian magpie. The scientific name *tibicen* means 'flautist', but in this case it is a thoroughly intoxicated flautist who has decided to add gurgles, giggles and slurs. The song of the magpie has been transcribed as 'Quardle oodle ardle wardle doodle', in a famous poem by New Zealand poet Denis Glover, but the truth is that it is one bird song that is virtually indescribable.

Scientifically the song is exceedingly complex, not just in output but in the physiology involved. The sound-producing organ of a bird is the syrinx, situated at the junction of the two branches (bronchi) of the lung at the base of the windpipe. This means that a bird song is not a single voice, but two voices: the composite of the flows of the left and right bronchi. The song of the Australian magpie is known to feature elements from just the left flow, just the right flow, and both flows at the same time.

GOLDCREST
Regulus regulus

European folklore titles this little wonder 'king of the birds', hence his scientific name, *regulus*. He resides in coniferous woods and forests in much of Eurasia; northern populations move south in winter, for example to southern Europe and China.

Most people automatically assume that the wren is the smallest bird in Britain and Europe, but that title goes to the goldcrest and its closely related cousin, the firecrest. These species are among the smallest songbirds in the world, just 9cm (3½in) in length and weighing in at just 4.5–7.0g (¹/₅oz), the equivalent of a small denomination coin. Both are hardy, but the fact that the goldcrest occurs close to the Arctic Circle, even in winter, is truly astonishing. It is able to do this partly by cuddling up to other members of its species at night.

Its survival at such latitudes owes much to its ecological niche. Its sheer minuteness allows it to feed in places into which no other bird can squeeze, among the needles of coniferous trees. It can creep in even after snowfall, and by taking an endless supply of diminutive food items, such as springtails, aphids and mites, it can keep its inner fires burning. Tests have shown that a goldcrest can survive in a temperature of -35°C (-31°F) for 18 hours if sufficiently fed, maintaining a body temperature of 39–41°C (102–106°F). Not bad for a tiny ball of feathers.

PEREGRINE FALCON
Falco peregrinus

Found in a variety of habitats worldwide, this magnificent bird is thought to be the fastest in the animal kingdom.

The world's most admired bird, perhaps, the peregrine is undoubtedly the fastest, and is also one of the most wide-ranging, and can be seen just about everywhere except Antarctica and the Amazon, in every habitat and in every climate. It can be found from Arctic deserts to the centres of large cities. It is a bird that kills birds, in unrivalled variety and prodigious numbers.

The peregrine's fame rests mainly upon the astonishing speeds that it can reach during one of its signature dives, from a height (known as stoops). There are so many estimates of its maximum speed that it is hard to be sure what is reliable, but at the very least it can dive earthwards at 165km/h (just over 100mph). This probably pips other speedsters such as hummingbirds and swifts. The stoop, dropping almost vertically on prey, finishes with the peregrine hammering the quarry with its talons, leading at the very least to the target becoming unbalanced; it is often disabled and sometimes killed instantly. The stoop is only one of the peregrine's many hunting methods; it can grab prey from underneath and creep up on unsuspecting birds to catch them by surprise.

Arguably, the peregrine's versatility is truly its most remarkable asset. Serious estimates of the number of bird species taken range from hundreds to about 2,000 species. The latter amounts to one-fifth of the world's birds. They are all terrorized by this single, astonishing predator.

MISTLE THRUSH
Turdus viscivorus

Mistle thrushes stake their claims on berry bushes round about now. They Breed in mosaics of wooded and open country, in Europe and Asia east to Himalayan foothills; may retreat from northern parts of range in winter.

At this time of the year, there are battles over berries going on. Listen out for a harsh rattling sound: this will be a mistle thrush getting hot under the collar.

Mistle thrushes are unusual among European thrushes for their habit of taking control of long-lasting berry clumps, such as holly and mistletoe, and defending them from other birds. The idea is that one or a pair of mistle thrushes utilizes their bulk and aggression to requisition these berries as a larder in case of hard times later in the winter. It's a living store on a tree or shrub, rather than a hidden cache.

So long as they defend it successfully, the thrushes can access berries right through the winter.

COMMON MYNAH
Acridotheres tristis

Native to warm parts of Asia; widely introduced, to Australasia, southern Africa, Madagascar and many other islands.

A glimpse into the future today. What new bird might one day take over the world, in the manner of a house sparrow, feral pigeon or collared dove, riding on the coat-tails of humanity?

Here's a strong candidate. Indeed, in the year 2000 it was declared one of the world's most invasive species by the International Union for Conservation of Nature Species Survival Commission. Native to warmer parts of Asia, it has been introduced to an eclectic set of locations, from the continent of Australia to isolated oceanic islands, such as Mauritius. It thrives in hot countries and does particularly well in suburban and urban environments. Pairs make a nest in a hole in a tree, and they are increasingly developing a reputation for driving native species out of cavities.

As the climate warms, so the mynah can spread further. It could be *the* bird of the 21st century.

BLACK SWAN
Cygnus atratus

Black swan pairing. These birds are found in all kinds of wetlands throughout Australia; introduced to New Zealand.

This Australian swan is the black sheep of the swan 'family'. This is confirmed when it takes off, betraying the gleaming white of its wings, and its heritage. The amount of white in the wing varies between the sexes, with more in the male. During courtship, the male lifts its wings.

These birds have an extraordinary display just prior to copulation. Both birds lower their heads and necks so that they are parallel to the water's surface, and then repeatedly dunk them into the water. They may repeat this action, with short breaks, for up to 25 minutes. Copulation takes place and then the birds enact a triumphant ceremony by stretching their necks upwards. Homosexual pairings are quite regular, and they also enact this unusual pre-copulation ritual.

One of Australia's early explorers, British naval surgeon George Bass, was unimpressed by the black swan's call, saying that it 'exactly resembled the creaking of a rusty ale-house sign on a windy day.'

LIVINGSTONE'S TURACO
Tauraco livingstonii

A uniquely
coloured bird of
eastern Africa
from Tanzania to
South Africa.

It will come as a surprise to most people to learn that not many birds are green. Many do appear green, it's just that they aren't actually green – at least, their don't contain any green pigment. Most green in birds is a combination of yellow pigment overlaying feathers whose structures reflect blue. One group that does have green pigments, however, is a spectacular family of African birds called turacos. They have two unique, copper-based hues, turacoverdin (green) and turacin (red) found nowhere else in the animal kingdom.

COMMON HILL MYNAH
Gracula religiosa

Native to the
forests of eastern
India and much
of south-east Asia
and Sundas.

A denizen of the treetops of moist forests in south-east Asia, the
hill mynah might have lounged in obscurity if it were not for its
exceptional voice. Few birds make such a wide range of sounds at human
pitch. For centuries the vocal abilities of mynahs have made them popular
cage birds and those that make the best imitations of the human voice
– everyday phrases, whistles and single words – can fetch high prices.
Although protected in the wild, many thousands are illegally trafficked
every year for this purpose. The irony of the mynah bird's skill is that,
in the wild, it doesn't mimic other birds, but rather communicates
with others of its kind in a rich, varied and verbose rambling all its
own. One scientist has divided the calls into 'chip calls', 'um-sounds',
'whisper-whistles' and miscellaneous 'calls'. By the time he created that last
category, he had probably given up trying to describe the range of babbles,
shrieks and croaks made by this delightfully loquacious species.

EURASIAN CURLEW
Numenius arquata

Breeds on bogs, moors and tundra of Eurasia; migrates south in winter to coasts of much of the Old World, except Australasia.

Y ou cannot mistake the curlew due to its long, curved bill. One of the largest of the shorebirds, it is also one of the most distinctive.

But what is the bill for? Or, more pertinently, why is it curved and not straight? One of the main reasons is the turning-circle at the tip. If the curlew probed its bill through a gap, perhaps in the burrow of a crab, a straight bill would be restricted, whereas the curved tip can investigate around corners in search of prey. Secondly, it is easier to grasp food when probing above.

In that case, why don't all shorebirds have noticeably curved bills? Well, there are disadvantages, too. A curved bill is more liable to break, so it must be strengthened internally with a series of struts. The gap at the tip of the bill is too narrow for the tongue, so the curlew cannot swallow some food items until they have been brought to the surface.

WILLIE WAGTAIL
Rhipidura leucophrys

This is a real bird that behaves as if it is battery-operated. A live wire, it moves around with jerky steps, flies in expansive zig-zags, darts to and fro, and constantly wags and fans its tail. It is the 'shepherd's companion', one of the most common birds of the Australian countryside. On a constant lookout for flies and other insects, it will perch on the back of livestock, hoping to catch something flushed from the grazer's feet. Its constant motion and cheerful demeanour has endeared it to people all over the continent.

22ND NOVEMBER

GRANDALA
Grandala coelicolor

It should be everybody's dream to see a flock of grandalas, since this is arguably one of the most beautiful sights in the entire ornithological world. Related to thrushes, grandalas have a deep cobalt colour all of their own. In the autumn, in the Chinese and Himalayan uplands, they gather in large flocks, many hundreds strong, to feed on berries.

INDIAN PEAFOWL
Pavo cristatus

It's so familiar that we often overlook the display of the Indian peafowl. In purely visual terms it must be the world's greatest. The number of 'eyes' on the train (which is not the tail but the feathers below the tail) may be as many as 150, and as far as females are concerned, the male with the most wins. Females visit on multiple occasions and tot them up.

You might expect such an exotic creature to be a rare forest bird, but go to India and they are everywhere, from agricultural fields to parks and temples. This is partly because they are sacred to Hinduism. In Hindu art, the Lord Krishna is invariably depicted with peacock (the male) feathers in his crown. Many Hindu deities are also portrayed riding on the backs of the birds.

MURPHY'S PETREL
Pterodroma ultima

Breeds at the moment on South Pacific islands including Pitcairns, Tuamotu archipelago, Austral islands and Gambier islands, possibly Easter Island. Wanders widely across the eastern Pacific.

Male and female Murphy's petrels share incubation of their single egg. The male begins, sitting for about 19 days, and then the female takes over for the next stint. The egg hatches after 50 days, about halfway through the male's second stint.

What might you think the off-duty parent might do in the meantime? The answer is to wander off somewhere to have a good feed. In the case of the birds breeding on Henderson Island, in the Pitcairns, that means a quick takeaway to the north-east to the waters of the Humboldt Current, off Peru and Chile.

Nothing remarkable about that, you might say – except that their off-duty wanderings can take them in a loop of 15,000km (9,300 miles)!

RED CROSSBILL

Loxia curvirostra

In conifer forests throughout North America and Eurasia; also northern Central America.

We take it for granted that we are right-handed or left-handed; it is just a part of life. So perhaps we shouldn't be surprised to learn that some birds exhibit a similar trait.

The crossbill, a finch, is unique among birds for having mandibles that cross over one another. This is an adaptation for extracting conifer seeds from cones. To feed, it inserts its bill tip between the scales of the cone and then, by shutting its bill, prises them apart.

Young crossbills in the nest, fed by the adults, have straight bills, but after a month or so the lower mandible begins to bend so that it crosses the upper – but it has to cross either to the left or the right. It turns out that about 50 per cent of crossbills have their mandible twisted to the left, and 50 per cent to the right.

KING PENGUIN
Aptenodytes patagonicus

Breeding
starting now
on subantarctic
islands, South
Georgia east
to Macquarie;
also Falklands,
south Chile.

In the human world, a king is lower in the pecking order than an emperor, but is still very impressive. So it is with the king penguin, the smaller and less extreme relative of the emperor penguin. Although it is not as large and doesn't breed as far south on inhospitable ice shelves, it is still amazing.

It has the longest breeding season of any bird in the world, taking 14–16 months to raise a chick from the laying of the egg, which includes the whole winter during which the chick may fast for 5 months. This penguin can also dive up to around 300m (1,000ft) deep, down into the darkest water. Its favourite food is lantern fish, which are bioluminescent, so presumably this helps the penguins to see them.

MALACHITE SUNBIRD
Nectarinia famosa

The adult male malachite sunbird is metallic green. His lady is brown and yellow. They reside in the grassland, mountain scrub and fynbos of southern Africa and northward patchily to parts of East Africa.

Sunbirds come in an array of glittering colours and feed on nectar. Does that sound familiar? If you are thinking hummingbirds, that's it; the sunbirds are their equivalent in the Old World.

One very big difference between sunbirds and hummingbirds, though, is that sunbirds perch to drink from flowers, while hummingbirds hover, beating their wings at a phenomenal rate to hold their bodies still in the air so that they can manoeuvre their bills into the blooms of tubular flowers. Intriguingly, most bird-pollinated plants in Africa and Asia provide perches conveniently near their blooms so that the sunbirds can reach them.

However, in recent years, a plant introduced from South America to southern Africa called tree tobacco has started to change sunbird behaviour. As there is nowhere to perch, some individuals have started to hover to reach the flowers. So sweet and rich are these blooms that the malachite sunbird is starting to embrace the New World fashion.

EURASIAN SPARROWHAWK
Accipiter nisus

Resident in most of Europe, almost any habitat; populations of northern Europe and Asia migrate south in winter, as far as East Africa and southern Asia.

To many people, the presence of a sparrowhawk at a feeding station is upsetting. In truth, it is merely evidence of a healthy bird population in a garden or neighbourhood. This pint-sized raptor is a true specialist: it is a hunter of birds and almost nothing else. It catches them by ambush, first concealing itself on a perch while watching their comings and goings, planning its method of attack according to the amount of cover, the number in the flock and the open-ground distance between itself and its prey. It approaches silently, hoping to catch birds off-guard, often using obstacles to obscure its approach (moving cars and even people can be used to screen an attack). The final ambush is a talons-first, headlong rush.

Female sparrowhawks are much larger and heavier than males (200–350g/7–12oz as opposed to 100–200g/3½–7oz) and take bigger prey on average. A bird eating a starling, thrush or pigeon will be a female, while males prefer to eat tits, larks and finches.

WILD TURKEY
Meleagris gallopavo

A bird most famed for its flavour, the turkey is native to open, mature deciduous forest over much of North America, south to central Mexico.

Every year, North Americans eat more food on Thanksgiving Day (the fourth Thursday in the month in the USA) than on any other day, and the centrepiece for the feast is roast turkey. The choice is significant, because the wild turkey is only found in North America and is therefore a genuine native and iconic bird. It is, indeed, the only bird from the western hemisphere that has become a choice meat elsewhere in the world.

The bird itself is a highly elusive inhabitant of open forest. Despite its size it is secretive, and it both runs and flies well, at great speed. By day it feeds mainly on the ground, but at night it roosts high in trees, sometimes as much as 16m (52½ft) above the forest floor. Its shy demeanour, sharpness and palatability also make it a great favourite among the hunting community.

WHITE-NECKED JACOBIN
Florisuga mellivora

Above: Found in the tropical evergreen forest of Central and northern South America.

Top right: Native to Eurasia and North Africa, pigeons occur in cities and towns worldwide.

Bottom right: Forests of Amazonia and northern South America.

If there is such a thing as the definitive hummingbird, perhaps the white-necked jacobin is a good fit. It is, after all, one of the most widespread of all the 300 or so species, occurring from Central America right across the Amazon Basin and south to Bolivia. It is colourful, a mixture of pure white and iridescent green and blue. It is relatively tiny, just 11–12cm (4½in) in length, and it has a long, very thin bill, with which it drinks nectar while hovering at flowers. A classic humming bird.

The white-necked jacobin also possesses another hummingbird quality in spades. It is downright bolshie. Wherever they are, these birds are aggressive. They bicker at clumps of forest flowers and they bicker at hummingbird feeders in rainforest lodges. They would start an argument on their own at a single bloom. Hot temper is a hummingbird trait through and through.

ROCK DOVE/FERAL PIGEON/TOWN PIGEON
Columba livia

Apparently (and somewhat bewilderingly), one of life's great mysteries (at least according to the Internet) is: why do you never see baby pigeons?

The answer is that young pigeons remain in the nest until they grow to adult size. After it hatches, the pigeon squab stays put, fed by its parents, until it is about a month old. By then it looks so similar to an adult pigeon that people don't realize they are looking at a youngster.

PURPLE HONEYCREEPER
Cyanerpes caeruleus

Have you ever seen legs like these – yellow on an iridescent blue body? The purple honeycreeper looks exactly like an exotic tropical bird, and that is precisely what it is, with its main home being the lowland Amazonian rainforest. Here it eats insects, nectar and fruit in the middle and upper storeys, but it simply cannot resist visiting the bird tables at eco-lodges where fruit and other goodies are put out for the birds.

If you see this in the wild, you are in a very pleasant place indeed.

BLACK KITE
Milvus migrans

Happy to get food where they can, even from humans, black kites thrive in open country and watersides throughout the Old World; the populations in north of Eurasia migrate south.

It is tempting to think that, when the apocalypse eventually comes, all life on earth will be destroyed – except for the black kite. If ever a bird seems indestructible, thriving everywhere from the depths of wild forests to the urban hub of Delhi, it is the world's most numerous raptor. In some ways the black kite is more human than humans – bold, inventive, risk-taking, cheeky, adaptable and everywhere. There is a population in the rubbish tips near the Indian capital that holds about 100,000 birds, each fed on people's waste.

The black kite is a mixture of the supreme and the subprime. In the air it rivals many a raptor, with its twisting tail and long wings conferring sublime aerial skills. However, it has little or no ability as a predator, and instead dallies with the dead, the decayed, the destroyed and the disdained.

HOODED PITOHUI
Pitohui dichrous

The poisonous pitohui is common in forests on the island of New Guinea.

Who's heard of a pitohui? Not many people have. It is a forest bird found in New Guinea, quite handsome but nothing special. To be honest, the pitohui would be lounging in the depths of obscurity if it wasn't for one extraordinary characteristic – it is poisonous. This species and a couple of its relatives are the only poisonous birds in the world.

The native New Guineans are unimpressed, labelling pitohuis 'rubbish'. That, though, is the idea. The plumage and skin contain batrachotoxins, the same deadly toxins found in arrow-poison frogs. The more rubbish the pitohui's flesh is, the better protected it is from predators, and the happier the bird will be.

WHITE BELLBIRD
Procnias albus

This obscure, but attractive pure-white bird of the forests of north-east South America, has recently been shown to have the world's loudest song. It is a slightly buzzy, bell-like sound 't-TONG' with a mechanical feel. It has been recorded at 125 decibels.

Repeated exposure to such a loud sound, equivalent to a pile driver, could be damaging to the ears. It certainly carries across the forest canopy.

LAYSAN ALBATROSS
Phoebastria immutabilis

Same-sex pair bonds are rare in birds, but they do happen. In colonies of Laysan albatrosses in Hawaii, the overall sex ratio is three females to every two males, so some females pair up together instead. One individual copulates with a male and the two females share the incubation and feeding of the chick. If successful, the pair bond can be long-lasting, with females taking turns laying the egg. One partnership is known to have lasted 19 years.

Above: A cheerful sight in eastern Australia. Introduced to western Australia.

Top left: Tall forests of Guinea Shield in north-east South America; small population in Amazonian Brazil.

Bottom left: Breeding now on Hawaii and islands off Japan and north-west Mexico; wanders widely over the North Pacific.

RAINBOW LORIKEET
Trichoglossus moluccanus

The comings and goings of rainbow lorikeets are a part of the daily spectacle for many city dwellers of eastern Australia. These gorgeous birds commute, but in the opposite direction to working people. They gather in large roosts inside the city at night, and then, during the day, they fly out to the countryside in search of flowering trees, particularly gum trees. In addition, they are abundant garden birds, for example in Sydney, where they can be trained to come to the hand to feed and to bird feeders.

Their main sustenance, though, is derived from nectar and pollen. Lorikeets have unusual tongues with extrusions at the tip called papillae, creating a brush-like surface that mops up nectar very quickly using capillary action. Their guts are also thin-walled because nectar is so easy to digest. Lorikeets can obtain what they need for an entire day in just a few hours.

GYRFALCON
Falco rusticolus

The gyrfalcon's main issue is climate change and the pergines moving in with the warmer weather. They inhabit tundra and coasts of the Arctic, across Eurasia and North America. Northernmost populations retreat south in winter.

It's the whitest death-chase in the world: the High Arctic gyrfalcon, resplendent in white flecked with black, pursues the all-white ptarmigan in winter plumage against a backdrop of ice and snow. It might be all but invisible, until the ptarmigan starts to bleed.

The gyrfalcon is the world's largest falcon (falcons are birds of prey with sharply pointed wings, long tails and a 'tooth' on the bill used to slice the spinal cord of prey). It is also the world's hardiest, breeding further north than any other bird of prey, in the Arctic of North America and Eurasia.

The gyrfalcon is also unusually choosy when it comes to diet. While its relative the peregrine falcon eats thousands of species, the gyrfalcon usually just chooses one. Ptarmigan can account for 90 per cent or more of an individual's diet.

CAPE SUGARBIRD
Promerops cafer

A male caped sugarbird, perched on his favourite flower – a protea. Found in gardens, coastal scrub and fynbos of South Africa.

Sugarbirds are only found in South Africa. They take advantage of an extraordinary phenomenon, perhaps the greatest concentration of flowers in the world. The Cape Floral Region is home to 8,600 species of plant, enough to fill an entire continent. Many of these grow in the fynbos, scrubby country of which the signature bloom is the protea.

The protea is the sugarbirds' go-to flower; an individual might visit 300 blooms a day to feed on nectar. Sugarbirds also hunt for invertebrates in the branches of the protea, they place their nests inside protea bushes, and for the nest lining they use protea down. Even their migrations are protea-related – they move around as different species of protea flower in different places at different times of year.

RUFOUS-TAILED JACAMAR
Galbula ruficauda

These 25cm (10in) birds have 5cm (2in) bills for snatching up insects. They are found in the forest edges and clearings of Central and South America.

With all those marvellous butterflies flying around the tropical forests of Central and South America, you might have wondered who their predators are. The answer is the jacamars, a small family of emerald beauties closely related to kingfishers, who feed on them exclusively. They sit on an elevated perch and wait for one to pass, snapping it up in flight.

There are hordes of butterflies, but the jacamar's problem is that some are edible and some inedible. The edible ones tend to fly fast and on an unpredictable course. The inedible ones are often very colourful and fly slowly. Their colours are a warning sign that they are worth avoiding; their slow flight demonstrates their confidence that they will not be caught. If a jacamar eats a butterfly with this so-called aposematic colouration, it will be suitably traumatized.

However, in the jungle there are also cheats. These are gourmet butterflies that have nevertheless evolved to look like the poisonous ones, thus deceiving hunters into leaving them alone.

But it turns out these cheats have underestimated the jacamars. The birds have an eye for extraordinary detail. The cheats might look like unpalatable species, but here and there is a speck, a spot or a suspicious pattern that differs from the original, even in a minute way. Amazingly, experienced jacamars can tell them apart, using their extraordinary powers of instant identification to see through their disguise.

Above: A coterie of noisy miners mobs a kookaburra. Found in open woodland and edge habitats in eastern Australia.

Top right: Breeds (at the moment) on riverine shingle in New Zealand's South Island; winters on estuaries on North Island.

Bottom right: A hunter of voles and rodents across North America and Eurasia.

NOISY MINER
Manorina melanocephala

One of the most common birds in eastern Australian suburbs and open woodland, the noisy miner has one of the most complicated social lives of any bird in the world. Birds of a specific neighbourhood live in a male-dominated grouping of 6–25 birds known as a 'coterie', which is a long-lasting social assemblage. Coteries often mix with birds from a number of other coteries in a large, loose colony that may contain 200 birds, all of which associate from time to time, for example to mob predators. Males in one or more coteries will sing together in 'corroborees'. Within social groupings birds will roost and feed together.

Male members of a coterie will help a female member with feeding young in a nest. Up to 22 have been recorded visiting a single pampered brood, and rarely fewer than six. Why they should do this, when usually only one male inseminates the female, nobody has yet worked out.

WRYBILL
Anarhynchus frontalis

At first glance, the wrybill doesn't look like anything unusual, just another shorebird. But look closer and you will see that the bill bends to the right. It is the only bird in the world with a laterally curved bill, and it invariably bends in the same direction.

The unusual shape allows the wrybill to reach the larvae of caddis flies, mayflies and other invertebrates under rounded stones, which predominate in its breeding habitat, the riverine shingle of New Zealand.

GREAT GREY OWL
Strix nebulosa

The mighty great grey owl can survive and feed in the depths of an Arctic winter. Its hearing is so good that it can detect the movements of rodents under the snow. The mammals themselves are able to survive all winter feeding on vegetation and insulated under the snow. But they aren't protected from the owl's predatory skills. Great grey owls have been known to dive, clenched talons first, through 45cm (nearly 18in) of snow to procure their prey. Nowhere is safe for voles and pocket gophers!

KEA
Nestor notabilis

The playful kea is found in high altitude forest and clearings and some lowland coasts in South Island of New Zealand.

The kea of New Zealand is the only alpine parrot in the world, and by far the least vegetarian, frequently eating meat. However, its true claim to fame is its inherent playfulness.

Keas are forever chasing one another, both in the air and on the ground. They will toss objects forwards and back, as if they are playing catch. They will wrestle for no reason. They are insatiably curious, investigating anything interesting and often destroying it or taking it away. One reputedly stole a tourist's passport at a ski resort. They like to chew car tyres and interfere with tents. They have been observed sliding down the sides of tents, as well as roofs, just for fun.

Remarkably, keas also have a 'laughter call', which will induce a playful response in other individuals – it is infectious. Aside from humans, only chimpanzees and, astonishingly, rats demonstrate contagious emotion. The super-intelligent kea is the only bird known to do so.

BLUE JAY
Cyanocitta cristata

Related to magpies and rooks, these birds are pretty, clever and devious. They live in all kinds of forests in eastern North America, also parks and gardens.

The 'Jaaay' call of this bird is one of the most common and evocative sounds of North America, a staple in the soundtrack of hundreds of movies and TV shows. The bird itself is fabulously coloured and is a regular visitor to bird feeders, delighting many and annoying some as it monopolizes the handouts.

The blue jay also has an unusual distinction; it quite often uses deception, one of the few birds to do so. Its wide vocabulary includes excellent mimicry of several predatory hawk species. It is thought that, when faced with large numbers of other birds at a feeder, a blue jay simply uses its talent to pretend to the feeding birds that there's a raptor on the loose. The spooked birds scatter, leaving the bird table free for the cunning jay.

347

RED-VENTED BULBUL
Pycnonotus cafer

In the 19th century these bulbils were kept in cages and often as fighting birds. Now they are found in the forests and gardens of India and adjacent southern Asia.

Go anywhere in the warmer parts of Africa and Asia and you will come across a family of birds called the bulbuls. The name might derive from the simple, repetitive but very cheerful vocalization, but the term 'bulbul' also refers to the nightingale of Europe, and can be used as a general term for a bird with a good voice – indeed, in the Arab world good human singers are sometimes called 'bulbuls'. Such an association flatters the real bulbuls, none of which (there are over 100 species) is exactly a virtuoso.

The red-vented bulbul is a common species in India and other parts of Asia, where it thrives in human environments, including gardens. Noisy and sociable, it feeds on fruit, berries, nectar, pollen and occasionally flowers.

This species has been introduced to other parts of the world, including Hawaii, where it is abundant, and several Pacific islands. It flourishes because of its easy association with humans.

BOHEMIAN WAXWING
Bombycilla garrulus

At home in boreal forest and muskeg across North America and Eurasia; migrates south, periodically in large numbers.

The Bohemian waxwing might just have the key to sartorial perfection. There are few birds in the world that, regardless of time of year, weather or circumstance, look so smartly presented. No individual deviates from the dress code; they are all turned out in neat, brownish pink, with a perfectly blow-dried crest, precise eye shadow, and colourful wing feathers glossed to perfection.

The secret could lie, as it often does, in what the bird eats. In this case, the waxwing's secret is the Total Fruit Diet. On an average winter's day this bird eats 600–1,000 berries, twice its body weight. It continues to eat sugary fruits all year round, adding in some flying insects, which it snaps up in mid-air, for extra protein.

It won't work for everybody, but in the waxwing's case the results speak for themselves.

CALIFORNIA CONDOR
Gymnogyps californianus

I n 1987, a momentous decision was taken over the fate of the California condor. Present in North America since the Pleistocene (2.5 million years ago until the end of the last ice age 11,700 years ago), this great scavenger had been declining for centuries, and was now critically endangered in its last outpost in southern California. A bird highly adapted to feeding on large carcasses, it was suffering from ingesting lead shot from hunters' bullets, which impaired its ability to fly and was often fatal. A bird with slow reproductive capabilities, time was nearly up on its presence in the modern world.

Conservationists decided to catch all the remaining wild birds, a total of just six, in an effort to start a captive breeding programme. But not all conservationists agreed. Many thought that the programme wouldn't work as the birds had never successfully reproduced in captivity. Others felt that captive-bred birds released into the wild would not survive for long. Some argued that it was better to let the birds die out. The disagreements led to much enmity and at least one fist fight.

The programme, though, has been a success. There are now around 400 California condors alive and about 200 have been released to several locations, even the Grand Canyon. The outlook remains as rocky as the environment however: the threat of lead poisoning hasn't gone away, survival rates are low and the project costs $5 million a year to run.

Above: Extinct in the wild but reintroduced into California, Arizona, Utah and Baja California.

Top right: Forests, edges and gardens from Central America and Caribbean to the south of Brazil.

Bottom right: Open habitats across Eurasia; northern and eastern populations highly migratory, wintering in Africa, Indian subcontinent and southern Asia.

BANANAQUIT
Coereba flaveola

The delightful bananaquit is something of a failed hummingbird. It has a strong love of nectar, but it doesn't hover. Instead it cheats by piercing the base of the corolla with its sharp, curved bill to get a sneaky sip. Common in the Caribbean, the bananaquit often patronizes outdoor bars and restaurants to take sugary treats from hummingbird feeders, plates or glasses. However, it has also acquired a taste for alcohol and – quite seriously – it has been shown to prefer 4–6 per cent proof, no more!

PIED (WHITE) WAGTAIL
Motacilla alba

It's not long until Christmas and in many parts of the world, houses, streets, town squares, malls and municipal buildings are adorned with outdoor Christmas trees, typically decorated with an array of colourful lights. Pied wagtails commonly come together and roost in the trees put up for Christmas, their thick foliage perfect as a place of shelter. It is possible, too, that these birds benefit from the faint microclimate created by the lights, which warm the air a little.

GALAH
Eolophus roseicapilla

Not a drunken hallucination, this really is a skyful of chattering pink birds. Only to be seen in Australia or New Zealand.

It's fair to say that the galah isn't much loved by the farmers and smallholders of Australia. In some quarters, to be called a galah is a term of abuse. These pearly grey and pink parrots, related to cockatoos, are naturally grain eaters, so it's hardly surprising that they flourish in agricultural areas and are only too grateful for the extra food. They abound over most of Australia, gathering together into substantial flocks, often in groups of more than 1,000.

It is regrettable than such a glorious bird is disliked or dismissed. Its pastel colours shine in the sunlight, and in the twilight, when flocks move to their roosts, they glow still more. The birds fly with deep wing beats, and characteristically sway from side to side as they go. Their distinctive call is a loud 'Chee, chee', with an odd quality that is hard to describe. But they are one of the sounds of Australia and, whether you like them or not, galahs are as Australian as the kangaroos that often graze near them.

COMMON GRACKLE
Quiscalus quiscula

Nests in dense evergreens in many habitats, including parks and gardens, across eastern North America, but wanders into many other habitats.

Not everybody likes grackles. They are sociable, noisy, inquisitive, a little brash and, in North America where they come from, so abundant as to be taken for granted. From backyards and roadsides to agricultural fields, they are everywhere, and although they are glossy, they aren't beautiful.

At this time of the year, though, grackles are amazing. At the end of each day, they gather together to roost, sometimes in enormous numbers. Fields can be thick with them and they swirl in the air like smoke. One grackle is no big deal, but a million grackles creates a marvel, and there are many such concentrations in the United States. They form one of the great avian spectacles on that continent.

COMMON POORWILL
Phalaenoptilus nuttallii

The poorwill is the only bird in the world that hibernates. It is a member of the nightjar family, a group of nocturnal birds with wide gapes that catch flying insects at night. This prey isn't easy to find when it's cold, so the poorwill avoids the winter's chill by spending months on end completely inactive. On any given day between December and February it will remain torpid, its body temperature reduced to close to that of its environment (as low as 5°C/41°F) and its oxygen consumption reduced by 90 per cent. Although many birds, including hummingbirds, often become torpid for short periods, especially at night, no other bird writes off the entire season. Poorwills have been known to be completely inactive for ten consecutive days.

Remarkably, the Hopi Indians have a name for this bird which reflects their knowledge of its torpor – 'The sleeping one'.

PARADISE TANAGER
Tangara chilensis

If ever a species epitomized the extravagance of the Amazon tropical forest canopy, it would have to be the paradise tanager. This gorgeous bird roams the tops of the trees in flocks of 10–20 individuals, searching for fruit and insects. These flocks often contain other multi-coloured species in the same family.

Tanagers are the songbirds that keep on giving in Central and South America. To see one is wondrous, to see many at the same time is one of the greatest gifts in all of birding.

EUROPEAN ROBIN
Erithacus rubecula

Every year, millions of Christmas cards, especially in the UK, are adorned with pictures of robins. A charming legend tells that the blood from Jesus Christ on the cross fell upon the bird's breast, staining it red (although that, of course, would have happened at Easter, in the spring).

Robins are unusual for their practice of pairing up in mid-winter, and singing, too – which is enough by itself to spread good Christmas cheer.

SECRETARY BIRD
Sagittarius serpentarius

This predator stalks the savanna and open grassland in much of sub-Saharan Africa away from forest belt.

With its wispy crest, long tail and greatly extended legs, the secretary bird has an almost comical look as it strides across the African savannah. However, it is a predator, and a very effective one; if you are a smallish mammal or bird, you would be advised to flee. If not, you are likely to be kicked to death.

The secretary bird is very unusual among birds of prey for catching most of its food on the ground. Sometimes it will encounter something as it is walking along, and at others it will run into the brush simply to flush out something edible. It will be attracted to bush fires and will ambush distracted prey trying to flee.

All are despatched by this bird's powerful feet, which are armed with heavy scaling. Its long toes are used to grab and to stamp on smaller prey until unconscious. Even quite sizeable prey, such as young antelopes or large snakes, can be kicked to death in a furious exhibition of lethal martial arts.

GIANT HUMMINGBIRD
Patagona gigas

Found in dry open country at all levels in the Andean chain of western South America.

At 22cm (8½in) long, 'giant' might be an exaggeration, bearing in mind that this is the same size as a Eurasian starling. However, in hummingbird terms it is the largest by some distance, twice as heavy as the next (the great sapphirewing). When feeding, its wings beat 'only' 15 times a second, just a quarter of the speed of some hoverers. Indeed, the wingbeats appear slow and deliberate, and when the bird is flying from place to place it will often glide at certain times.

The giant hummingbird has been found over an amazing altitudinal range, from sea level to 4,500m (14,760ft). It is found mainly in dry, open country, often feeding at cactus flowers. However, its favourite food plant is the *Puya*, a genus of high altitudes, an outsized, spiky bromeliad, with which the bird has a symbiotic relationship of feeder and pollinator. Some *Puya* species have flower stalks up to 10m (33ft) – so this hummingbird will not go short of food.

WHITE-THROATED DIPPER
Cinclus cinclus

This hardy bird braves the fast-flowing rivers and streams of Eurasia and North Africa.

The dipper is the world's only aquatic songbird, living a life of total immersion in fast-flowing streams. It has no obvious external adaptations to this extreme habitat, so you would never guess from a quick glance that it was anything unusual. However, it is portly, has exceptionally dense plumage, a large preen gland supplying it with waterproofing oil, and strong feet for clinging on to stones and rocks underwater. The dipper doesn't immerse itself by diving, instead it simply wades in and enters with barely a ripple. Once submerged, it fights its own buoyancy by 'flying' against the current and holding itself down with its feet. In the rapids it feeds on insects and their larvae, fish eggs and a few small fish.

In the roaring streams where it lives, communication is difficult, and this is thought to be why the dipper employs its dipping action, bobbing up and down when perched. It also has a white eyelid, which could also act as a visual signal.

Dippers are remarkably hardy, surviving in temperatures as low as -45°C (-49°F) as long as the streams don't freeze. It also sings and maintains territory from December onwards.

INACCESSIBLE RAIL
Atlantisia rogersi

With no predators but only a small population, this flightless bird clings on to all habitats on Inaccessible Island in the South Atlantic.

Let's hear it for impossible dreams. The Inaccessible Island rail is arguably the most difficult species to see in the world. Apart from birds that might be out there somewhere, but nobody knows where, this bird probably offers more challenges than any other.

Inaccessible Island forms part of the Tristan da Cunha group, in the South Atlantic, the most remote inhabited island group in the world, 2,432km (1,511 miles) from Cape Town in South Africa and 3,486km (2,116 miles) from the Falkland Islands, themselves 483km (300 miles) off the coast of Argentina in South America. It takes a week to sail from Cape Town, and few boats go there. Once you arrive in Tristan it is difficult to land and there's nowhere to stay. Then you must persuade somebody to take you to Inaccessible, 31km (19 miles) away, which is strictly protected.

The problems don't end there. Inaccessible Island lives up to its name. It is a high plateau above sheer cliffs, with just one landing beach. Only between December and January do you get much chance of landing, and in reality just a few days a year are suitable in this gale-blasted part of the world. Then you have to climb the cliffs, which are treacherous.

359

GREY HERON
Ardea cinerea

A loafer or an expert meditator? This 1m (40in) tall bird hangs around lakes, rivers and wetlands throughout the Old World apart from Australia; northern populations migrate south in winter.

On those long, winter days, have you ever felt like doing absolutely nothing, and staying in bed?

If you yearn for such a lifestyle, consider the grey heron. This bird is well known as the patient angler of the river bank, who wades into the water, then waits for a fish to come into range. After a while, the prey is grabbed and swallowed.

If the prize is a good one, the grey heron's needs are satisfied for much of the rest of the day. So, what is there to do? The answer is: nothing.

It finds a day roost, for example, on a tree branch or simply on the ground in a field, settles down and rests. It spends 17 per cent of the remainder of the day preening, just 6 per cent sleeping and no less than 77 per cent standing, perfectly awake, just loafing. Heaven!

EURASIAN JACKDAW
Corvus monedula

Resides in open country in Europe, east to Central Asia and in North Africa. Jackdaws practice food sharing, regardless of kinship – a seasonal lesson to us all.

Whilst many a mingled swarthy crowd –
Rook, crow and jackdaw – noising loud,
Fly to and fro to dreary fen,
Dull winter's weary flight again;
They flop on heavy wings away,
As soon as morning wakens grey,
And, when the sun sets round and red,
Return to naked woods to bed.

So wrote John Clare, the great English rural poet. It perfectly describes the winter comings and goings of jackdaws and other crows from the fields where they forage to their roosts in the woods.

Picture Credits

© Shutterstock pages 4, 28, 32, 35, 50, 58, 61, 63 bottom, 74 bottom, 79, 80, 82 top, 86 bottom, 94 top, 94 bottom, 95, 105, 107, 113, 119, 120, 126, 127, 128, 129, 144, 149, 156 bottom, 158 bottom, 165 top, 167, 168, 170, 177, 181, 189, 192, 196, 201, 208, 209, 213, 219, 223, 234, 235, 239, 240, 244, 245, 246 bottom, 247, 260, 261, 264, 273, 282, 290 top, 308, 311, 318, 325, 330, 334, 335, 339, 344, 349, 351 top, 354.

© Getty Images / ZU_09 page 7; THEPALMER page 8; Rick Friedman page 176.

© Hannah Dale, Wrendale Designs Ltd pages 14 top, 14 bottom, 15, 27 top, 48, 52, 56, 57, 68, 86, 97, 140 bottom, 161, 176, 205, 210, 263, 266, 271, 282.

© John Walters page 18.

© Alamy Stock Photo / AGAMI Photo Agency pages 20, 47 top, 183, 206 bottom, 224; agefotostock pages 43, 329; Alan Keith Beastall page 87; Albert Wright page 21; All Canada Photos pages 31 top, 109, 134, 307, 338 bottom, 353, 355 top; Ambling Images page 335; Andrew Digby page 243; Antiquarian Images pages 122 and 285; Archivist page 73; Archive PL page 142; Arco Images GmbH page 98 top; The Artchives page 254; Arto Hakola page 155 bottom; Asar Studios page 236; Auscape International Pty Ltd page 12; Barry Freeman page 54; Bill Coster page 216; Bill Gozansky page 125; BIOSPHOTO page 323; Birds page 82; Bird of Prey, Alius Imago page 62; blickwinkel pages 47 bottom, 53, 69, 91, 118, 138, 164, 283, 293; Blue Planet Archive page 309; Bob Gibbons page 190; bojangles page 92; Buiten-Beeld pages 137, 139, 140 top; Christian Hütter page 229; Christoph Bosch page 340; Chronicle page 204; Craig Churchill page 355 bottom; Cultural Archive page 130 and 207; Danielle Connor page 115 bottom; Danita Delimont pages 41 and 214; David Chapman pages 104 and 306 bottom; David Havel page 148; David Norton page 154; David Tipling Photo Library pages 31 bottom, 151, 163, 169, 269, 332; DBI Studio page 324; Design Pics Inc page 219; Dinodia Photos page 275; Don Johnston_BI pages 193 and 237 bottom; Ecolelogical page 356; Everett Collection Inc page 262; F1online digitale Bildagentur GmbH page 88; Fabrice Bettex Photography page 158 top; Farlap page 76; Florilegius pages 45, 81, 115 top, 251, 290; FLPA page 326 bottom; Frans Lanting Studio page 241; fStop Images GmbH page 166; Genevieve Vallee pages 278 and 300; George Ostertag page 258; Granger Historical Picture Archive page 96; Gregory Gard page 313; Harry Collins page 103; Harvey Wood page 25; Hemis pages 284 and 292; Heritage Image Partnership Ltd page 141; Historic Collection page 328; The History Collection pages 199 and 343; Iconographic Archive page 75; imageBROKER pages 108, 191, 233, 286, 314, 326 top, 341; Imogen Warren page 184; Ivan Kuzmin page 276; Ivan Vdovin page 83; Impan Art Collection (JAC) page 106 bottom; Jesse Kraft page 227; Jess Merrill page 77; John Quixley - Australia page 322; Juan Aunion page 203; Juanma Hernández page 24; Juha Jarvinen page 50; Kevin Ebi page 310; KEVIN ELSBY page 253 and 358; Keystone Press page 157 bottom; KIKE CALVO page 67; Lars S. Madsen page 99; Linda Kennedy page 66; Lynnette Peizer / Stockimo page 220; Malcolm Park

editorial page 133; Malcolm Schuyl page 291; manjeet & yograj jadeja page 44; Marc F. Henning page 165 bottom; Mark Bretherton page 287; Martin Fowler page 145; Martin Harvey page 222; Martin Lindsay page 26; Matthew Cuda page 93; Matthijs Kuijpers page 98 bottom; McPhoto/Schaef page 147; Meibion page 11; Michael Shake page 112; Michael Stubblefield page 206 top; Michelle Gilders page 10; MIHAI ANDRITOIU page 89; mike lane page 320; Minden Pictures pages 2–3, 46, 60, 151, 159, 171, 175, 187 top, 218, 295; Mint Images Limited page 114 and 231; Mircea Costina page 268; National Geographic Image Collection pages 72 and 85; The Natural History Museum pages 123 bottom, 131, 279, 348; Nature Picture Library pages 9, 19, 22–23, 33, 110, 111, 143, 172, 228, 248, 259, 274, 297, 303, 331, 336, 346, 368; Nature Photographers Ltd pages 155 top, 157 top, 162, 173, 182, 257; Neil Bowman page 294; Neil Walker page 74 top; Neftali page 230; Nick Gleitzman / Stockimo page 185; Nobuo Matsumura pages 37 and 337; North Wind Picture Archives page 246 top; Old Images page 71; Oldtime page 299; Olivier Parent page 360; Oliver Smart page 327; Oliver Thompson-Holmes page 242; Oscar Dominguez page 221; Pat Bennett page 306 top; Paul Farnfield page 215; paul weston page 304; Paul Young page 123 top; Peter Morris page 352; Phichak page 212; Philip Mugridge page 40; PhotoAlto page 136 bottom; Pictorial Press Ltd page 226; Premium Stock Photography GmbH page 198; Rafael Ben-Ari page 102 bottom; Ray Wilson page 102 top; Richard Berry page 17; Richard Tadman page 256; Rick & Nora Bowers pages 197 and 302; robertharding pages 150 bottom, 288, 305; Roberto Nistri page 30; Rolf Kopfle page 63 top; Samyak Kaninde pages 56 and 289; Sean McConnery page 345 bottom; Sergey Komarov-Kohl page 250; Sergey Uryadnikov page 321; Shubhashish Chakrabarty page 84; Simon Stirrup page 277; Stephanie Jackson / Australian birds collection page 29; Steve Taylor ARPS pages 200 and 217; tbkmedia.de page 13; Tim Graham page 249; Tim Plowden page 187 bottom; travelstock.ca page 238; USFWS Photo page 59; Vasiliy Vishnevskiy page 317; Victor Tyakht page 265; Walker Art Library page 117; Westend61 GmbH page 357; William Leaman page 211; Yakov Oskanov page 36; YAY Media AS page 42; YES Collection page 296; Zoonar GmbH page 134; Zvonimir Atletić page 34.

© The Bradshaw Foundation page 27.

© Kim Wormald – lirralirra page 51

© Madeleine Floyd pages 101, 267, 361.

© Nature Picture Library / Robin Chittenden page 152; Nick Garbutt page 194; Andrew Walmsley page 345; Troels Jacobsen/Arcticphoto page 359.

© Lonnie Bregman page 281.

© The Harry G. C. Packard Collection of Asian Art, Gift of Harry G. C. Packard, and Purchase, Fletcher, Rogers, Harris Brisbane Dick, and Louis V. Bell Funds, Joseph Pulitzer Bequest, and The Annenberg Fund Inc. Gift, 1975 page 298.

© Freer Gallery of Art, Smithsonian Institution, Washington, D.C.: Gift of Charles Lang Freer, F1909.245v page 312.

© Museum of New Zealand/Dick Frizzell; artist; 1987; Auckland page 316.

© Anselmo D'Affonseca, Instituto Nacional de Pesquisas da Amazonia page 338 top.

Further Reading

Cocker, Mark, *Birds and People* (Jonathan Cape; 2013)

Lovette, Irby J. (editor) and Fitzpatrick, John W (editor), *Handbook of Bird Biology* (Wiley-Blackwell; 2016)

Gill F., D Donsker, D. and Rasmussen, P. (Eds). 2020. IOC World Bird List (v10.1). doi : 10.14344/IOC.ML.10.1.

Birds of North America (BNA) Online at birdsna.org

Neotropical Birds Online at neotropical.birds.cornell.edu

Handbook of Birds of the World at www.hbw.com

INDEX

ACKNOWLEDGEMENTS

A book of this kind could not exist without the largely unseen army of scientists and researchers who are forever coming up with remarkable discoveries out there in the wild. My first acknowledgement should be to them.

Many thanks are due to Tina Persaud at Pavilion Books for commissioning this work in the first place, and for Kristy Richardson and the team at Batsford for picture research and for making the work coherent – no mean feat, and requiring a great deal of hard work and dedication.

Finally, writing a book can be an effort not just for an author, but also for their family. My heartfelt thanks to my wonderful wife Carolyn and children Emmie and Sam, who have to put up with listening to random facts about birds at the kitchen table and elsewhere.

The extraordinary and rarely glimpsed blue bird-of-paradise (see page 274).